THE SECOND BOOK OF IRISH BALLADS

The Second
Book of Irish Ballads

EDITED BY

JAMES N. HEALY

THE MERCIER PRESS LIMITED
4 BRIDGE STREET, CORK

First published 1962
© Mercier Press Limited Cork

Printed by
Bosch, Utrecht, Holland

To
M

ACKNOWLEDGMENTS

Many people have helped me with this book – some only by singing the songs in a delightful way when I first heard them at all stages of my life; and others helped in a more practical way in helping me with lost words and tunes and these include – Dan O'Keeffe, 'Poochey' Lynch, Sean Feehan, Mick Gill, James Ryan, Tom Finn, Siobain O'Brien, Mary Healy, Paddy O'Connell, to these and to others who have helped in any small way, grateful thanks. Thanks is also due to the copyright holders for giving permission for the printing of words of which they hold the right; these include Piggot and Company (The Sive Song) the Misses French and the Keith Prowse Music Publishing Co (The Mountains of Mourne; Are ye right There Michael; Sweet Marie; Drumcollogher): thanks also to Charles Ginnane for reading the proofs.

Foreword

Books are written to be read; plays are made to be acted, and ballads are made to be sung. Unless a ballad is singable it might as well not have been written at all. The ballads in this book find their way in primarily because they have that quality, and only occasionally because of some literary or personal valuation.

There are many reasons, of course, why a particular ballad becomes popular at a particular time. It may be that the event described is topical, or that a singer has given a specially good performance of it; or it may be pure chance. Sometimes ballads which have been dead for years attain a sudden resurgence of popularity for no reason that can be satisfactorily explained, but in all cases a ballad will not last, or be revived, unless it has a quality that forces itself on the ear of the listener: it must be capable of being sung, simply, by ordinary people.

Very often old tunes, known around the countryside for years, have been utilised to provide the music for ballads and in that way some beautiful and very ancient traditional music has been preserved. In many cases these tunes are twisted around ingeniously to provide the proper mood for the ballad concerned: and it is worth noting how often some tunes have been used, in widely spread parts of the country, for different ballads, at different times.

This surely indicates how well this music must have been known in the instrumental or possibly earlier vocal versions throughout the country in olden times – for indeed some of it can be traced back for many hundreds of years. This does not say, of course, that every tune used in a ballad is of very old origin – few of the ballads we hear today are any older than the latter part of the eighteenth century, when English was beginning to replace Irish as the spoken tongue of the people: and indeed most of the ballads before the nineteenth century were written by men who could be recognised as poets, or by the sporting fraternity of the better-off classes.

Ballad writing in English first became a popular mode of expression in, and following the period of the United Irishmen and the Napoleonic wars.

From then on any incident was likely to provide the ballad-maker with a subject for his art.

Ballad makers, and ballad singers, can, one supposes, be accepted as being in line of descent from the Irish bards of older times; and indeed, the bardic tradition and the existence of the Seanacaidhe (native story teller) must have helped to establish the popularity of ballad singing, for, to some extent at least, it has taken the place of both.

The ballad is above all things the voice of the people, for in it they have expressed their feelings, sad and comic, cheerful and forlorn, at street corners, at home and in public houses, about a variety of things – politics, history, the death of a patriot, the loss of a loved one, a sporting event, ambushes, emigration, drinking, escapades and misadventures, curses for real or imagined wrongs, religion, love of a place of beauty; home.

The whole gamut of human feeling has been run in ballads – some of them very beautiful in their simplicity; some contrived and artificial; some fiercely patriotic, others comically twisting grim events.

Feeling is important in a ballad – some of the apparently trivial have survived on this score: so is rhythm and a set of words which flow easily. It is important that the music selected suits the words and the theme, or is adapted to suit them – happy examples of this are 'Carrigdhoun' (page 32) and Percy French's 'The Mountains o' Mourne' both of which use the same basic tune, but in different ways. It is given a sad, haunting quality in the first, omitting some of the notes used in the version for the second song: for which it provides a livelier setting for the wryly-comic words, without losing the nostalgic quality.

The authorship of many ballads cannot be traced. More often

than not they were written by people who had no regular claim to be writers, or in circumstances which made a claim to authorship indiscreet at the time.

On the other hand recognised writers have turned their hands to ballads, or at the least to lyrics later accepted as ballads, and some of these are included in the present collection.

Generally speaking, however it has been thought preferable to include as many as possible which have not appeared in print before, or at least have not done so for some considerable time.

In setting out this book every effort has been made to give due credit to authors and arrangers, when the information could be obtained; and the claim was genuine, but there are, of course many unavoidable gaps. If any acknowledgments have been omitted which should have been made we are more than sorry, and hope to be excused.

When making selections of this type of music it is inevitable, of course, that personal preference enters into the choice, and that personal preference is often coloured by nostalgia.

I am a Corkman, and, as I am proud of it there are no apologies to make for that! This fact does mean however that I am better acquainted with the balladry of my own neighbourhood and environment that than of any other: and that therefore the collection includes rather more from Cork City, Cork County and Munster, than might be usual. Since many of these have not been printed before, however, I imagine, and hope, that readers from other regions will accept my choice.

In fact one could make up an entire book of ballads from the City and County, which I was almost tempted to do since the present choice meant leaving so many good ones out. Perhaps, however, it might be possible to include them in a future collection.

At any rate I have tried to give you a collection of ballads which you and your friends will want to sing: and if my choice helps you to pass some pleasant evenings around a piano together at least I will have achieved something.

22nd January, 1962   James N. Healy

Index

SONGS FROM THE IRISH

Ballads from Cork City

Like almost all centres in Ireland Cork City and County has many ballads and ditties peculiar to itself. Some of these such as 'The Banks', 'The Holy Ground' or 'Thady Quill' – have become so well known as to be considered national songs: many others have never been set down in print and are therefore generally known only in the district where they were first heard.

Others again were written many years ago and are now only to be found in out-of-print collections, or by word of mouth from one of the older generation by whom they have been preserved.

There are still more, such as the riotous 'Boys of Fair Hill' which were originally written for a specific purpose unknown to those singing it today. Where I have information on such songs I have noted it down, hoping that it might make them even more interesting to those who sing them; but no doubt they will bring particular reminiscences to many readers who already know the original story behind them.

Many of these ballads are either in the forthright, somewhat cynical humour of our capital of the south, or strong with the sentiment which its peoples love (although they will not always admit it!) Some of them achieve their best effect when heard in the broad sing-song accents of the City and may therefore be incomprehensible to one or two of you from outside it, but they are truly songs of the people, and should be preserved amongst the nations balladry. Recognised writers, such as John Fitz-Gerald 'The Bard of the Lee', or 'Father Prout', contributed a few, others are so old, or so obscure, in their origin that it would be impossible to say who the real author was.

Words Unknown: attributed by some to a Mr. Culleton
Music: arranged by J. C. Shanahan

How oft do my thoughts in their fancy take flight,
To the home of my childhood away,
To the days when each Patriots vision seem'd bright,
Ere I dream'd that those joys should decay,
When my heart was as light as the wild winds that blow,
Down the Mardyke through each elm tree,
Where I sported and played 'neath each green leafy shade,
On the Banks of my own lovely Lee.
Where I sported and played 'neath each green leafy shade,
On the Banks of my own lovely Lee.

And then in the spring-time of laughter and song,
Can I ever forget the sweet hours,
With the friends of my youth, as we rambled along,
'Mongst the green mossy banks and wild flowers.
Then, too when the evening sun sinking to rest,
Sheds its golden light over the sea.
The maid with her lover the wild daisies pressed,
On the Banks of my own lovely Lee.
The maid with her lover the wild daisies pressed,
On the Banks of my own lovely Lee.

Oh, what joys should be mine ere this life should decline,
To seek shells on the sea-girdled shore,
While the steel-feathered eagle, oft splashing the brine,
Brings longing for freedom once more,
Oh, all that on earth that I wish for or crave
Is my last crimson drop be for thee.
To moisten the grass of my fore-fathers' grave,
On the Banks of my own lovely Lee.
To moisten the grass of my fore-fathers' grave,
On the Banks of my own lovely Lee.

This song has become the anthem of Cork. One of the characters, in John B. Keane's play 'Many Young Men of Twenty' says 'If you stand in the middle of London any night and shout 'Ech-oah', every man that turns his head will be a Corkman': well, it could similarly be said that if you sang 'The Banks' loud enough anywhere in the world a Corkman would come running from somewhere, echoing the chorus, and, one would hope, with a bottle in his hand.

It was originally written as an emigrant song, as the last verse quoted above (but very seldom sung) indicates. Its origin is not definite. It has at times been attributed to John FitzGerald, the Bard of the Lee, who did *not* write it, and also to other sources; one of the stories is that it was written by a bankclerk named Culleton, who is supposed to have sung it with a colleague for the first time at a fancy dress ball, to the adaptation of a German tune by the Cork musician, J. C. Shanahan: the latter's family later preserved it for future generations of Corkmen (there will be such things despite the exodus to Dublin!) by arranging its publication.

No party of Corkmen, or women, would be complete nowadays, after the chimes of midnight, without it; and it has often brought tears to my own eyes, even if only twenty miles from Cork. On such an occasion somebody asks 'What about the Banks?', and there we are, singing our heads off. What matters its origin, as long as the song is there? Some ballad enthusiasts have noted its similarity to a ballad of rather more ancient vintage, written of a spot not so far from the City – 'Mount Massey the Pride of Macroom'.

Words and Music: Traditional

I long to remember those bright days of joy
Which sweetly with joy I beguiled,
The friends who frequented my old cabin floor;
And comrades I loved when a child.
How I longed for to roam, by Mount Massey's green groves,
Or poach by the light of the moon,
That spot of my birth, there's no equal on earth
Mount Massey, the flower of Macroom.

Chorus:
So friends come with me, and 'tis there you will see
The apples and cherries in bloom,
And 'tis you I'll invite, where I first saw the light
In Mount Massey, the flower of Macroom.

In the sweet summer time, when the season was fine,
What fun would be there at the gate,
The colleens would smile as they sat on the stile,
While the sweethearts their love tales relate.
When dancing was over, we'd stroll through the park,
Each lad and his lassie in bloom,
That spot of my birth, there's no equal on earth
Mount Massey, the flower of Macroom.

So now I must roam, from my own Irish home,
And cross o'er the wild raging sea,
To leave friends behind, both loving and kind,
And the colleens who dearly loved me.
'Tho fortune may smile far away from the isle,
I shall pray that the day will come soon;
When I'll stray once again, by that lovely domain
Mount Massey, the flower of Macroom.

3. BEAUTIFUL CITY

Words: John Fitz Gerald
Air: 'Beautiful Venice'

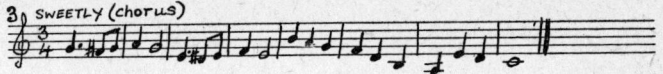

I have sought to discover a haven of rest,
Where the sun sinks by night in the land of the West;
I have dwelt with the red man in green forest bowers,
Or the wild-rolling prairie, bespangled with flowers;
I have hied to the north, where the hardy pine grows,
'Mid the wolf and the bear, and the bleak winter snows;
I have roamed through all climates, but none could I see
Like the green hills of Cork, and my home by the Lee.
Beautiful city, beautiful city,
Beautiful city, the pride of the Lee.

I have slumber'd in palm-groves by clear running streams,
And the wild groves of Blarney come haunting my dreams;
I have listened to bells on the soft summer wind,
But the sweet Bells of Shandon were dear to my mind;
I have mixed in gay dances my sorrow to hide,
But there's none like the maiden that's now by my side.
There is nought in the land of the slave or the free
Like the green hills of Cork, and my home by the Lee.
Beautiful city, beautiful city,
Beautiful city, the pride of the Lee.

The bold feudal castle looks down on the Rhine,
That flows through the land of the olive and vine;
There's freedom and health in the fresh mountain breeze,
That careers round the home of the brave Tyrolese;
There is beauty and love in all spots of the earth

To the heart that can call it the land of its birth;
But of all the fair countries, the dearest to me
Are the green hills of Cork, and my home by the Lee
Beautiful city, beautiful city,
Beautiful city, the pride of the Lee.

This song was originally written as 'The Green Hills of Cork'
and is one of a type of song popular in FitzGerald's time – the
exile longing to return to his native land. John FitzGerald was
born in 1825 and died in 1910. He was variously known as 'The
Bard of the Lee' and 'The Cock o' Sinbarry's'. After an early
education at the North Monastery he followed a variety of
trades before settling down at the School of Art as instructor of
woodcarving, an art at which he excelled. He loved Cork, and
wrote about the City in a great volume of verse. Some of it may
seem a little stilted to our ears, written as it is in the phraseology
of the last century; and some of the references, topical in Fitz-
Gerald's time, are now obscure because of the changes which
have been made in the City; but then these references have an
historical interest in themselves, if only because the customs and
places referred to in them are no more. With regard to the senti-
ments of 'Beautiful City', FitzGerald, to be sure, lived in
Cork all his life, except for a period in London when he was
young; but then most of the sad songs about exile were written
by people who never left the country at all – it is, in fact, sur-
prising how few really good ones have come from real exiles.
They may have been too busy making good in their new life to
get down to writing songs!

This song is a favourite nowadays in many a pub on a Saturday
night, particularly one in Barrack Street, and is rendered by
Corkmen who have never left the City, and hope they never will.

What harm: it is the sentiment which matters rather than the
words, and the gentle air, properly performed, has a soft nostalgic charm which has kept it alive for four generations.

Words: 'Father Prout'
Air: The Groves of Blarney (Traditional)

With deep affection
And recollection
I often think of
   Those Shandon bells,
Whose sounds so wild would,
In the days of childhood,
Fling round my cradle
   Their magic spells.
On this I ponder
Where'er I wander,
And thus grow fonder,
   Sweet Cork, of thee;
With thy bells of Shandon,
That sound so grand on
The pleasant waters
   Of the river Lee.

I've heard bells tolling
Old 'Adrian's Mole' in
Their Thunder rolling
   From the Vatican
And cymbals glorious
Swinging uproarious
In the gorgeous turrets
   Of Notre Dame;
But thy sounds were sweeter
Than the dome of Peter
Flings o'er the Tiber,
   Pealing solemnly.
Oh! the bells of Shandon
Sound far more grand on
The pleasant waters
   Of the river Lee.

I've heard bells chiming,
Full many a clime in,
Tolling sublime in
   Cathedral shrine;
While at a glibe rate
Brass tongues would vibrate;
But all their music
   Spoke naught like thine.
For memory, dwelling
On each proud swelling
Of thy belfry, knelling
   Its bold notes free,
Made the bells of Shandon
Sound far more grand on
The pleasant waters
   Of the river Lee.

There's a bell in Moscow
While on tower and kiosk O!
In Saint Sophia
   The Turkman gets,
And loud in air
Calls men to prayer
From the tapering summit
   Of tall minarets.
Such empty phantom
I freely grant them;
But there is an anthem
   More dear to me –
'Tis the bells of Shandon
That sound so grand on
The pleasant waters
   Of the river Lee.

'The Bells of Shandon' is now probably the best-known of a number of songs written to the same beautiful Irish melody, although the one which follows, about Blarney, was at one time more famous.

Although one can never be really sure when 'Father Prout' had his tongue in his cheek he seems to seriously praise the Bells, and show his real affection for the City which lies underneath. Certain it is, that at the end of his time 'Prout' really was an exile; so that the nostalgia is probably very real in his case. Shandon steeple, prominent over the Northern bank of the River Lee was built in 1722, and its faces of sandstone and limestone have watched the changing of the City for over two hundred years, during which time it has become one of the most famous landmarks. One of the 'must do's' in Cork for a visitor is to go and ring the famous bells. This can be arranged in the Church itself.

Nowadays the City is full of noise and bustle, but the ringing of the bells must really have dominated the scene in the quieter days of the reverend versifier.

The first two verses are particularly sweet sounding, and, with the tune, are nicely suited for four-part choral singing.

'Father Prout' was the pen-name of the Rev. Father S. Mahony, a member of the well-known Blarney family. He wrote a great deal of verse, and died in Rome in 1866.

The original, and at the time more famous, song written to this air was the satirical 'Groves of Blarney' written by Richard A. Milliken near the end of the 18th century. Milliken, a Bohemian of the time, ran a little theatre on the site of the present premises of the 'Cork Examiner', and later, another in Tuckey Street, where one of his company was the famous (or infamous as the thought may be) Harriet Smithson – a young Cork girl who later became a famous beauty on the continent and married the French composer Berlioz. He died in 1815.

The air of the 'Groves of Blarney' was in all probability taken from Slan Cois Maighe (Farewell to Maigue) which was written by Andreas Mac Crait, known as An Mangaire Sugac (The Merry Peddler), from the Maigue district of Limerick. This

Bohemian character was one of a circle of the Irish poets and writers around the middle of the 18th century and friend of Sean O Tuama (An Grian) who at that time owned a public house in Croom.

5. THE GROVES OF BLARNEY
Words: R. A. Milliken
Air: adapted from 'Slan cois Maighe (Traditional)

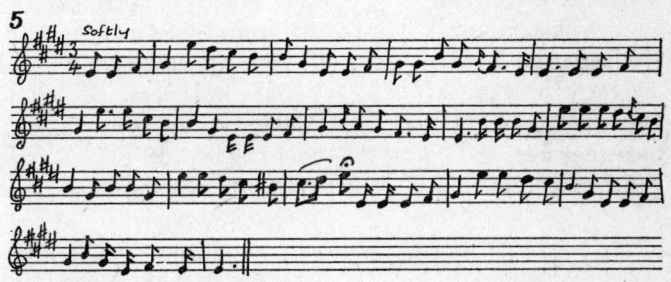

The groves of Blarney	'Tis Lady Jeffers

The groves of Blarney
They look so charming,
Down by the purling
  Of sweet silent streams;
Being banked with posies
That spontaneous grow there,
Planted in order
  By the sweet rock close,
'Tis there's the daisy
And the sweet carnation,
The blooming pink,
  And the rose so fair;
The daffodowndilly –
Likewise the lily,
All flowers that scent
  The sweet fragrant air.

'Tis Lady Jeffers
That owns this station;
Like Alexander,
  Or Queen Helen fair;
There's no commander
In all the nation,
For emulation,
  Can with her compare,
Such walls surround her,
That no nine-pounder
Could dare to plunder
  Her place of strength;
But Oliver Cromwell
Her he did pommell,
And made a breach,
  In her battlement.

There's gravel walks there,
For speculation,
And conversation
   In sweet solitude.
'Tis there the lover
May hear the dove, or
The gentle plover
   In the afternoon;
And if a lady
Would be so engaging
As to walk alone in
   Those shady bowers,
'Tis there the courtier
He may transport her
Into some fort, or
   All under ground.

For 'tis there's a cave where
No daylight enters,
But cats and badgers
   Are for ever bred;
Being mossed by nature,
That makes it sweeter
Than a coach-and six,
   Or a feather bed.
'Tis there the lake is
Well stored with perches,
And comely eels in
   The verdant mud;
Besides the leeches,
And groves and beeches,
Standing in order
   For to guard the flood.

*(additional verse later written
by 'Father Prout')*

There's statues gracing
This noble place in –
All heathen gods
   And nymphs so fair;
Bold Neptune, Plutarch,
And Nicodemus,
All standing naked
   In the open air!
So now to finish
This brave narration,
Which my poor geni
   Could not entwine;
But were I Homer,
Or Nebuchadnezzar,
'Tis in every feature
   I would make it shine.

There is a stone there,
That whoever kisses,
Oh! he never misses
   To grow eloquent;
'Tis he may clamber,
To a lady's chamber,
Or become a member
   Of parliament:
A clever spouter
He'll soon turn out, or
Anout-and-outer,
   'To be let alone,'
Don't hope to hinder him,
Or to bewilder him,
Sure he's a pilgrim
   From the Blarney stone!

Moore used the melody of 'The Groves' for 'The Last Rose of Summer' but changed it somewhat. The references to 'Lady Jeffers' and 'Oliver Cromwell' are in jest. The Castle was for a time in possession of the Jeffers family but, although it was 'pommelled' several times, Cromwell, of hated memory, was not, in this case at least, the culprit.

Blarney Castle is, of course, one of the most famous of the ancient castles in Ireland, if not in the world; and the fame of the 'Blarney Stone', which gives supposed eloquence to all who kiss it in its precarious position at the top of the building, brings flocks of people to climb the rugged and ancient steps every summer. Even if they do not become rewarded with a silvery tongue, the view from the top is worth it.

The legend originally arose during the time of Queen Elizabeth when the then holder of the property kept putting off with excuses her request that he should do something about the rebels, with whom he had a secret sympathy. She described his silken talk as 'All Blarney', and sometime during the following years it came to be believed that his eloquence had arisen from the possession of a magic stone which he had incorporated in the walls of the castle.

Before 'Prout' wrote the 'Bells' song he wrote a broadly comic version to the same tune called 'The Town of Passage' which followed two previous versions on 'Passage', the original by Simon Quin, who was a lodger with 'Molly Bowen'. Of these I feel that the simplest and best was the original and it is this I quote.

6. THE TOWN OF PASSAGE

Air: The Groves of Blarney (Traditional)
Words: Simon Quin

The town of Passage
Is neat and spacious,
All situated
  Upon the sea,
The ships a-floating,
And the youths a-boating
With their cotton coats, on
  Each summer's day.
'Tis there you'd see,
Both night and morning,
The men-of-war with
  Fresh, flowing sails,
The bould lieutenants,
And the tars so jolly,
All steering for Cork
  In a hackney chaise.

There's a ferry-boat
That is quite convenient
For man and horse
  For to take a ride,
And 'tis there in clover,
You may cross over
To Carrigaloe,
  At the other side.
There may be seen, o!
  The sweet Marino
With its trees so green, o!
  And fruit so red,
And lovely White Point,
And right forenent it
The Giant's Stairs,
  And ould Horse Head.

'Tis there's the strand, too,
That's deck'd with oar-weeds,
And tender gob-stones.
  And mussel shells;
And there's skeehories,
And what still more, is
Some comely, fresh
  Flowing water rills.
'Tis there the ladies,
When bread of day is,
Their tender lovers
  Do often pelt,
While some are airing,
And some are bathing,
Quite unadorned,
  To enjoy their health.

There's a house for lodgers,
At one Molly Bowen's
Where often goes in
  One Simon Quin,
Where without a coat on,
You'd hear him grope on
The door to open,
  And let him in;
Then straight up stairs –
One pair of windys,
With the slates alone
  'Twixt him and the sky,
Oh! 'tis there till morning,
The fleas all swarming
Do keep him warm
  Where he does lie.

Passage, Monkstown and Glenbrook stand closely together a few miles from Cork on the right bank of the River Lee as it winds its way to the open sea. They are 'just around the corner', so as to speak, from the broad expanse of the harbour where lies, on the other bank, Cobh ('Queenstown') where so many emigrants got their last glimpse of old Ireland.

White Point is a little beach on the Cobh side, not far from the new shipyards. The Giants' Stairs opposite are supposed, by legend, to enclose the remains of the Giant O'Mahony.

The last verse is reminiscent of François Villon – 'Ballade de la Grosse Margot' 'tho the bawdiness of the French poet is not, perhaps, intended.

This ditty can have absolutely no claim to literary elegance, but no collection of songs in which Cork is represented would be complete without it. Fair Hill stands just outside the City of Cork to the north, and in the long off days of about forty years ago the district boasted an enthusiastic hurling team of its own who used to present a colourful sight as they paraded down from Fair Hill on match days, mounted on the traditional jarvey cars, and singing with great voice the strains of the song which follows. For a good many years they had a successful career in junior ranks and then in 1918 decided to try their luck as seniors. Drawn in what might be termed the easier half of the competition, they beat firstly, 'Redmonds', and then 'St. Marys' to reach the final. Then however, came a long wait before they could take the field against their re-doubtable opponents – Blackrock, (the 'Rockies' of the song); as during these troubled times hurling and certain other sports, which meant the gathering together of a large number of enthusiastics who might be national minded, were banned. They did not, therefore, meet Blackrock until 1922, and in the intervening time this song came into full flower, and at all the matches, friendly or otherwise, (before the championship final) it was sung. The Fair Hill supporters formed together in a special part of the Athletic Grounds and kicked their heels with great vigour against the corrugated fencing whenever their team got a score, at the same time giving full vent to the chorus of this song. It is said to have been written by Sean Callaghan, a member of the club. It is rather a sad end to the story, therefore, to record that in spite of all the enthusiasm, Fair Hill were decisively whacked by Blackrock in the final – a defeat which meant the end of the club. They subsequently amalgamated with St. Marys who themselves later went out of existence, but the song has endured and has since been adopted as a belligerent challenge by all Cork men on the rampage.

Words and Music: Sean Callaghan

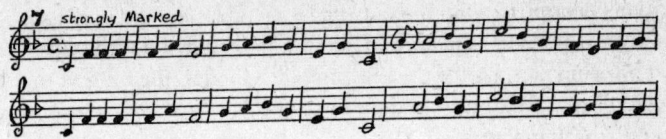

Come and have a holiday
With our hurling Club so gay,
Your souls we will charm and your hearts we will thrill:
The Boys they won't harm you,
The Girls all will charm you –
Heres up 'em all says the Boys of Fair Hill.

A hurling Club in a Fishing Village,
That does no fishing and much less tillage,
Thought that they could never be knocked out.
De Rockies thought they were the stars
'Til they met the Saint Finn Barrs,
But we bate'em all says the Boys of Fair Hill.

They searched the County upside-down,
They searched the City round de town,
Trying to bate us but dey got de'r fill.
They brought 'em from Tipperary bogs
And dressed them up in Redmonds Togs
But we 'flogged their nobs' says the Boys of Fair Hill.

The above is the original version. Since the purpose for which it was written, to cheer and encourage the hurlers of Fair Hill has been largely forgotten the song has been perpetuated by way of many couplets which bear little or no resemblance to the original purpose and indeed were not included by the original author. In fact, one of the traditions attached to the song in many gatherings is that it goes the round of the room, with everybody contributing a verse.

Here are some of those most often heard, but since verses are often added extemporaneously, and afterwards retained in the circle in which they have first been heard, or in the general tradition, one could never boast of recording a complete version.

> De Valera crossed de foam
> Jus' to kiss de Blarney Stone
> Here's up 'em all said de boys of Fair Hill
> Shandon Steeple stands up straight
> De River Lee flows underneaght
> Here's up 'em all said de boys of Fair Hill
>
> If you want to join our club
> Come right down to ... pub
> Here's to 'em all, said de boys of Fair Hill
> Dey sells rashers and drisheens
> Murphy's Stout and Pigs Crubeens
> Here's to 'em all, said de boys of Fair Hill
>
> Blackpool girls are very rude
> De go swimmin' in de nude
> Here's to 'em all said de boys of Fair Hill
> But den de are no good at all
> Up again de Sunbeam Wall
> Here's to 'em all said de boys of Fair Hill

. . . . hooked the ball
We hooked . . . . . ball and all
Here's to 'em all said de boys of Fair Hill
Blarney Hins don't lay at all
And whin de lays de lays 'em small
Here's to 'em all said de boys of Fair Hill

To my mind it is worth recording these extra verses of the song for the beautiful and contradictory statement about the Blarney Hens alone. The verse about the 'Hooker' has found its way in via the rugby clubs of the City who have a great affection for the song and have largely adopted it. The 'Hooker' varies from team to team, but was, originally, I think, 'Starry' Crowley who played for Constitution in the 'forties and 'fifties. In the hurling sense it has been applied to the great Christy Ring, and indeed to others before him.

Drisheens are that rare Cork delicacy, dried Sheep's blood, enclosed in part of the intestines – which sounds pretty gruesome but, decked out with white parsley sauce, is, in fact, quite delicious. Pigs Cruebeens are pigs feet, something I could never stomach myself, but a great favourite late at night with pints of stout.

Ballads from County Cork

8. THE HOLY GROUND

Just as 'The Banks' has become the Anthem of Cork, the Holy Ground has become the Anthem of Cobh, the pretty little seaport town of Cork Harbour. It is not originally an Irish song, since it was first heard of in Swansea, in Wales: but it has become so much a part of the scene down South that it cannot be considered out of place in an Irish songbook. There is, in fact, a district in Cobh known as 'The Holy Ground' at the Eastern end of the town, and it is, or was, the part where most of the seagoing population dwelt; so that the song is most appropriate to its present place of adoption. It is a drinking song, have no mistake about that and when Southern folk, particularly the Yachtsman element, get to the part where all stamp their glasses on the table and yell out together 'Fine Girl you are', it would shake the heart of any invader. It has certainly caused the breaking of many a glass.

THE HOLY GROUND
Words and Music: Welsh tradition

Adieu my fair young maidens, a thousand times adieu,
We must bid good-bye to the Holy Ground, the place that we
[love true;
We will sail the salt seas over, and return again for sure,
To seek the girls that wait for us – In the Holy Ground once more.
Fine Girl you are,
You're the girl I do adore,
And still I live in hope to see,
The Holy Ground once more – fine girl you are.

We're on the Salt Sea sailing and you are safe behind
Fond letters I will write to you, the secrets of my mind,
Fond letters I will to you, the girl I do adore
And still I live in hope to see the Holy Ground once more.
Fine girl you are,
You're the girl I do adore,
And still I live in hope to see,
The Holy Ground once more – fine girl you are.

I see a storm arising, I can see it coming soon
For the night is dark and dreary, you can scarcely see the moon
And the good old ship she is tossing about, and her riggings
                                                              [is all tore,
But still I live in hope to see the Holy Ground once more.
Fine girl you are,
You're the girl I do adore,
And still I live in hope to see,
The Holy Ground once more – fine girl you are.

And now the storm is over and we are safe on shore
And a health we'll drink to the Holy Ground and the girls we do
                                                              [adore
We will drink strong ale and porter, and make the taprooms roar
And when our money is all spent we will go to sea once more.
Fine girl you are,
You're the girl I do adore,
And still I live in hope to see – The Holy Ground once more –
                                        fine girl you are! –

Denny Lane, who died in 1899, was one of a circle of Cork poets who contributed much to the literature of the last century. Much of his work was lyrical, but Carrigdhoun provides us with an excellent ballad which has only recently become generally known again. It is the story told with simple sadness of a girl whose young man has gone off to the wars and left her behind, pining. A story often told, perhaps, but seldom with such quiet sincerity and lack of hysteria. In this case she is unlikely to see him again for he had gone to join the 'fleur-de-lis, – the Irish Brigade fighting with the French forces. Many Irishmen following the defeat and flight of Sarsfield's Wild Geese in 1691 accepted voluntary exile as a price of their freedom and left the country to become mercenaries in the armies on the Continent. 'Aghadoe' by John Todhunter is a similar type of song, but about a different period – it concerns the death of a lover shot by the redcoats during the Fenian times or before. Both are sweet songs all too rarely heard nowadays and if the publication of this book will help in having them sung more often at least one hope will have been achieved. The air to Carrigdhoun is an old one and was used by Tom Moore for 'Bendermeer Stream'. It has also been used, although not quite in the same form for a very popular song of Percy French's which has been imitated many a time since – 'The Mountains o'Mourne'; but the plaintivness of the original air is much more evident in Denny Lane's song.

CARRIGDHOUN
(lament of the Irish Maiden)

Words: Denny Lane
Music: traditional

The heath is green on Carrigdhoun,
The sun is bright o'er Ardnalia,
The dark green trees bend trembling down,
To kiss the slumb'ring Ownabwee.
That happy day, 'twas but last May,
'Tis like a dream to me,
When Donal swore, aye, o'er and o'er,
We'd part no more, asthore machree.

On Carrigdhoun the heath is brown,
The clouds are dark o'er Ardnalia,
And many a stream comes rushing down
To swell the angry Ownabwee.
The moaning blast is sweeping fast
Thro' many a leafless tree,
And I'm alone, for he is gone,
My hawk is flown, ochone machree!

Soft April showers and bright May flowers
Will bring the summer back again
But will they bring me back the hours
I spent with my brave Donal then?
'Tis but a chance, for he's gone to France
To wear the fleur-de-lis
But I'll follow you, my Donal Dhu,
For still I'm true to you, machree.

10. THE MOUNTAINS O'MOURNE

Words: Percy French
Music: traditional arr. Collisson

Oh, Mary, this London's a wonderful sight,
Wid the people here workin' by day and by night;
They don't sow potatoes, nor barley, nor wheat,
But there's gangs of them diggin' for gold in the street –
At least, when I axed them, that's what I was told,
So I just took a hand at this diggin' for gold,
But for all that I found there I might as well be
Where the mountains o'Mourne sweep down to the sea.

I believe that, when writin', a wish you expressed
As to how the fine ladies in London were dressed.
Well if you'll believe me, when axed to a ball,
They don't wear a top to their dresses at all.
Oh, I've seen them myself, and you could not in thrath,
Say if they were bound for a ball or a bath –
Don't be startin' them fashions now, Mary Macree,
Where the mountains o'Mourne sweep down to the sea.

I seen England's King from the top of a'bus –
I never knew him, though he means to know us;
And though by the Saxon we once were oppressed,
Still, I cheered – God forgive me! – I cheered wid the rest.
And now that he's visited Erin's green shore,
We'll be much better friends than we've been heretofore,
When we've got all we want we're as quiet as can be,
Where the mountains o'Mourne sweep down to the sea.

You remember young Peter O'Loughlin of course –
Well, here he is here at the head o' the Force.
I met him to-day, I was crossing the Strand,
And he stopped the whole street wid wan wave of his hand;
And there we stood talking of days that are gone,
While the whole population of London looked on;
But for all these great powers he's wishful, like me,
To be back where dark Mourne sweeps down to the sea.

There's beautiful girls here – oh, never mind!
Wid beautiful shapes Nature never designed,
And lovely complexions, all roses and crame,
But O'Loughlin remarked wid regard to them same:
'That if at those roses you venture to sip,
The colours might all come away on your lip.'
So I'll wait for the wild rose that's waitin for me
Where the mountains o'Mourne sweep down to the sea.

This is one of the best constructed of the ballads I have come across dealing with the period of the 'Black and Tans'. The engagement described is one typical of the time: and there is a logical strain to the account which rings very true. Moreover the country wherein the ambush is described – the wild mountainy district around Kilcorney and Nadd, twenty miles or so to the north of the City – is particularly suited to this type of guerilla warfare. It is only fair to note, however, that I, personally, can find no record of any such engagement having ever taken place. Nevertheless, this is a very fine ballad of its type which has not, to my knowledge, been printed before.

THE KILCORNEY AMBUSH

Words: 'G.M.'
Air: 'The Boston Burglar'

My name is Willie Reardon from Curraragge I hail,
Five years I fought for Ireland's cause, and ten in England's gaols.
The Black & Tans and Auxies too had reason to relate
The many fierce engagements in which I did participate.

Cross Barry's famed in history; Kilmichael's famed in song,
But Kilcorney's fame is in hearts aflame for Ireland's cruel wrong;
And if you listen to me now, a story I will tell,
Of the bloody fray that day in May by Kilcorney's rugged dell.

'Twas long before the Dawning we were ready in the glen,
And Commandant Sean McCarthy he whistled up his men;
But twenty strong we gathered there, our weapons in our hands,
And listened to our leader calling out his bold commands.

We had rifles ten and shotguns eight, and two had hand-grenades,
Myself and Long Tim Lenihan the hero of many raids,
There was Sullivan and Jacky Lane, whom we laid in hero's
[graves,
Sure they died for flag and country that we never might be slaves.

We quickly took positions the sun now shone on high,
And gleamed upon the faces of the men all set to die
And shed their blood for Erin's cause beneath an Irish sky:
From many a lip a muttered prayer soon sped to heaven on high.

The youngest of our gallant band, 'twas he first saw the foe,
In 'Lancy-cars' and lorries on the dusty road below,
'Steady boys' our Leader cried and no man moved his head,
'I'll give the word' no sound was heard save the lorries heavy
[tread.

Then suddenly on that bright May morn the battle's roar was
[heard,
And Ireland's guns rang out once more to take revenge in lead.
The enemy were halted, their leader soon fell dead,
And ere our last round found its mark, the rest of them had fled.

To Crinaloo and Inchamay and on to Caherlow,
The news soon spread, the day was won and twenty Tans laid
[low.
Oh silently we laid our dead in the little church that night,
And turned bravely to the morn to carry on the fight.

This song first saw the light of day in the latter part of the 18th century. Mallow is a busy town twenty miles from Cork on the main road to Limerick and was then fashionable as a Spa, and a gay resort for young people of society who had little to do with their leisure but spend it. The writer was very likely one of the young set of his time who scribbled the lines off for the enjoyment of his friends at a party, not realising that they would filter through the succeeding years; which they have so well that the tune, originally known by another name is now invariably called 'The Rakes of Mallow', even if the words (which are not so easy to sing) haven't been remembered so well. From my young days I remember an additional verse but I don't think it was part of the original – it is an interesting addition, including as it does the towns encircling Mallow in this fertile part of Cork County – the area of County houses in which the 'Rakes' would circulate

> Mallow, Tallow, Cappoquin
> Doneraile and Charleville
> Breaking windows up and down
> Hurrah! for the Rakes of Mallow town.

It is of somewhat the same style, and period, as 'Garryowen' another song of which the tune is now better known than the words and both may have been sung in the same spirit as the 'Boys of Fair Hill' is to-day – although in a different strata of society.

At the time there was also a famous Spa near Limerick – at Castletroy, and the doings of the boys of Garryowen would approximate to those of Mallow. (For the words of 'Garryowen' see the first Mercier Book of Ballads, collected by Dan O'Keeffe)

THE RAKES OF MALLOW

Words: attributed to Edward Lysaght
Air: 'Sandy lent the man his mule'

Beauing, belling, dancing, drinking,
Breaking windows, damning, sinking,
Ever raking, never thinking
Live the rakes of Mallow.

Spending faster than it comes,
Beating waiters, bailiffs, duns,
Bacchus' true begotten sons,
Live the rakes of Mallow.

One time naught but claret drinking,
Then like politicians thinking
To raise the sinking funds when sinking,
Live the rakes of Mallow.

When at home with dadda dying,
Still for Mallow-water crying;
But where there is good claret plying
Live the rakes of Mallow.

Living short but merry lives,
Going where the devil drives,
Having sweethearts, but no wives,
Live the rakes of Mallow.

Racking tenants, stewards teasing,
Swiftly spending, slowly raising,
Wishing to spend all their days in
Raking as at Mallow.

Then to end this raking life
They get sober, take a wife,
Ever after live in strife,
And wish again for Mallow.

Kildorrery, perched on the top of a hill on the road between Mallow and Mitchelstown, is eulogised in a slightly satirical way in this lively ballad, which has a great similarity to one by Percy French on Drumcollogher, which by the way of contrast follows. The aims are nearly the same, although the emphasis is somewhat different.

KILDORRERY

Words and Music unknown

1. I've been to a great many places
   Ballycotton, Tramore and Tralee
   Ballybunion and all other places
   And all the resorts by the Sea.
   For my health I have travelled thro' Ireland
   Till now I'm at last settled down,
   Tho' lacking in wealth, I've recovered my health
   Since I came to Kildorrery Town.
   Chorus:
   Have you ever been down to Kildorrery
   If you haven't now isn't that queer.
   Sure its only five miles from Ardpatrick
   And three from the cross of Redchair
   Now when at that cross you are landed
   You'll see a big hill looking down
   And on top of that hill looking naked and chill
   Stands famous Kildorrery Town.

2. When St. Patrick came over to Ireland
   He said to the South he'd come down
   And where do you think he took lodgings
   But above in Kildorrery Town.
   And when on the way to Kilmallock
   St. Patrick he died on the way
   Those who stood by his side on the day that he died
   They heard him distinctly say

(repeat four lines and –)

Lay my bones on the hill of Ardpatrick
And there let my grave be laid down
And my soul in its flight, if it goes to that height
Will pass thro' Kildorrery Town.

3. When King Richard came over to Ireland
In delicate health as you know
I met him one day in my travels
And he asked me which road would he go
He said its fresh air that I'm seeking
As my spirit is truly run down
Well, King Richard, said I, if its fresh air you'll find
Its above in Kildorrery Town. (*Chorus:*)

4. When the Pilgrims went over from Ireland
Bound for fair Italy's shore
Little they knew what surprises
That fair land for them had in store.
They went to the Pope in his Palace
And when he had seated them down
He asked loud and clear is there anyone here
From famous Kildorrery Town.
Chorus
Said the Pope 'I was once in Kildorrery
Altho' you may think that is queer
But I went down the road by Ardpatrick
And on by the Cross of Redchair
So now I will give you my Blessing
So please on your knees all kneel down
May Prosperity smile on Erin's green Isle
And on famous Kildorrery Town.'

As a personal preference I think I prefer the Kildorrery Song – it has the feeling of having been written from inside so to speak; whereas Percy French's cheerful ballad has an external air – of having been written merely about a town, the name of which happened to come into his head. They are both rollicking songs, however, and well worth the singing.

DRUMCOLLOGHER

Words and Music: Percy French
Drumcollogher is a town in County Limerick.

I've been to a great many places,
And wonderful sights I've seen
From Aghernavoe to Ballinasloe
And back to Ballyporeen.
But when they talk of the towns that
Over the ocean lie –
When they say to me, 'Pat, what do you think of that?'
I ups and I says, says I –
Chorus:
I suppose you've not been to Drumcollogher?
Ye haven't? Well now I declare,
You must wait till you've been to Drumcollogher.
And seen the fine place we have there,
There's only one street in Drumcollogher,
But then 'tis a glory to see;
Ye may talk till you're dumb, but give me ould Drum,
For Drum is the place for me.

They tell me there's Isles of the Ocean
By India's golden shore,
Where life all day long is a beautiful song,
With flowers and fruits galore;
They tell me the sun does be shining,
With never a cloud in the sky –
But when they have done with their clouds and their sun,
I ups and I says, says I –
Chorus:
I suppose you've not been to Drumcollogher?
Ye haven't? Well now I declare,
You must wait till you've been to Drumcollogher,
And seen the fine sun we have there,
There's only one sun in Drumcollogher,
But then 'tis a glory to see;
Ye may talk till you're dumb, but give me ould Drum,
For Drum is the place for me.

I was over in London quite lately,
I gave King Edward a call;
Says the butler, 'He's out, he isn't about,
An' I don't see his hat in the hall;
But if you like to look round, sir,
I think you will have to say,
Apartments like these are not what one sees
In your country every day.'
Chorus:
Says I, 'Have ye been to Drumcollogher?
Ye haven't? Well, now I declare,
You must wait till you've been to Drumcollogher?
And seen the fine house we have there.
There's only one house in Drumcollogher,
For hardware, bacon and tea;
If your master would come we would treat him in Drum,
Oh! Drum is the place for me.'

From the Family Circle

Most people associate certain songs with their own youth, if they are lucky enough to have a family circle who indulged in the pleasant old habit of musical evenings. These evenings seem now to have been defeated by the wireless, cinema and that devouring beast, the Telly; but I was lucky enough, when very young, to have just got on the tail end of the wagon before they died out at home, and so I heard many numbers at that time which might never otherwise have come to my ears: in addition they gave me a fondness for songs and for singing for which I was grateful later on. There they were generally conducted by my grandfather, no mean hand at throwing off a ballad himself, and I only regret that some of his have passed from memory, so that I am unable to record them.

However I have preserved three, 'Ben the Coachman', 'The Goat' and 'The Bug-a-Boo' which may be of interest.

15. THE BUG-A-BOO

Words: traditional } arr. James
Air: 'Bug-a-Boo' } N. Healy

Come all ye tender and faint hearted blokes and a welcome
warning take from me,
   Until I narrate the dangers across on the mighty sea,
   Sure many is the toil and trouble, me bonny boys that I've been
thro'
   A-ship with the Steward and the Cook, me boys, aboard of the
Bug-a-Boo.

When first I saw the nate little craft she was in the Patrick Street
Canal,
   She looked so neat and trim, boys, forget her shape I never,
never shall,
   And the Captain he wore an old straw hat, knee-breeches and
a body coat of blue,
   He cut such an Elegant figure-head, me lads, to ornament the
Bug-a-Boo.

We sailed away till the break of day, and the sea ran mountains
high,
   And the lightning roared and the thunder flashed, and
wrenched the dark red sky,
   And the second mate he gave orders for us our sail to clew,
   And the Captain in his cabin was smoking his Dudeen, set fire
to the Bug-a-Boo.

When the Captain found out what he had done he loudly for
help did shout,
   Shure he bawled out thro' the chimney pot for the helmsman
to come and put it out,
   But the helmsman he was fast asleep, and we our sails did clew,
   And the fire got so far in the middle of the Terf, they couldn't
save the Bug-a-Boo.

We sailed away till the break of day to a latitude of forty-four,
And the poor Bug-a-Boo she burnt, me boys, until she
could'nt burn anymore,
And the Captain he gave orders to lower away the boat and
save the crew.
And a thousand sods of Terf and eleven Million Fleas went to
Blazes in the Bug-a-Boo,
And a thousand sods of Terf and eleven Million Fleas went to
blazes in the Bug-a-Boo.

I cannot claim this for my grandfather, but he certainly was one
of the first I ever heard singing it. I know he lent the words in the
late 'twenties and that it was subsequently recorded in the early
'thirties, both as a ballad, and a jazz number by an American
band. I broadcast it during the Real Blarney series.

It may originally have been a canal ballad which would lend a
satiric significance to the lurid description of the storm. To add to
this point I am following it up with a version of the 'Toor-al-i-
ay' theme on the same subject from the midlands.

16. THE BALLAD OF THE 13TH LOCK

Words: traditional
Air: 'Toor-al-i-ay'

Every night of the year, about twelve of the clock
The ghosts and the spooks of Draferteen flock
Sit swingin' their bodies all this and that way
And mournfully singin' 'Right Toor-al-i-ay'

There once was a Captain both gallant and bold
And he laughed at the warnings of young and of old
'Dye think' he'd remark and most scornfully say
'That I'd fear a dead ghost singin' 'Toor-al-i-ay'.'
Chorus:
Singin' Toor-al-i-oor-al-i, Toor-al-i-ay
Singin' Toor-al-i-oor-al-i, Toor-al-i-ay
And what would you do now, and what would you say
If you met a dead ghost singin' Toor-al-i-ay.

One Saturday night, coming home from Athy
He halted his boat as the lock he passed by
And he jeered as them ghosts sittin' there on the Quay
All mournfully singin' 'Right-Toor-al-i-ay'.

When he reached into Dublin his money was spent
So 'twas in to them manager's office he went
Says the manager nodding; 'A very fine day'
'H-m, H-m, H-m' (hum) says the Captain 'Right-Toor-al-i-ay.'
Chorus:
Singing, Toor-al-i-oor-al-i, Toor-al-i-ay,
Singing Toor-al-i-oor-al-i, Toor-al-i-ay
For the devil a word me bould Captain could say
Barring 'Toor-al-i, Toor-al-i, Toor-al-i-ay'

Well a day or two after he took to his bed
The Doctor was sent for but he shook his head,
For there's no such disease in the pharmacal way
That I ever heard tell of as Toor-al-i-ay.

The very next morning me bould Captain died
His wife and his childer around him they cried
And the last words he spoke when they axed him to pray
Was 'Toor-al-i, Toor-al-i, Toor-al-i-ay.'
Chorus:
Singing Toor-al-i-oor-al-i, Toor-al-i-ay.
Singing Toor-al-i-oor-al-i, Toor-al-i-ay.
And the last words he spoke when they axed him to pray
Was Toor-al-i, Toor-al-i, Toor-al-i-ay.

The tune of this ballad, which can best be called 'Toor-al-i-ay' is found in different versions all over the country, where local variations of the chorus are numerous and often widely different.

In its origin it is probably not Irish at all, as the earliest use of it which can be traced is the English 'Villikins and his Dinah'.

Waltz tempo became popular for ballads with the popularity of the waltz as a dance measure in the last century, and old Irish tunes were adapted to the tempo: on other occasions, as apparently in this one, tunes were borrowed from other sources. One of the most typical uses of this music is the Waterford ballad 'Master McGrath' (see Book of Ballads No. 1) which was written about a greyhound of that name which won the Waterloo Cup in 1868, 1869 and 1871. A memorial to 'The Master' has been erected at a crossroads near Dungarven.

During the late forties another greyhound was in the headlines.

"TOOR-AL-I-AY" VARIATIONS

16 (1) BALLAD OF THE 13ᵗʰ LOCK (EAST)

49

This was 'Quare Times' who was setting up 'quare times' on tracks here and in England. At that time I was one of those concerned in a Radio series called The Cork Melodymakers, and for one of their broadcasts in 1946 I wrote a version to the same tune. It was allied to a sketch in which Quare Times was pitted against the legendary Master McGrath, to the latters discomfort. This was in its own poor way a satire, I suppose, but many people wrote for the words at the time ,and later when it was again heard in a 'Real Blarney' programme, so here it is:

QUARE TIMES

Words: James N. Healy
Air: Master McGrath
(Toor-al-i-ay)

On Saturday night I went up to the track
With me dog be me side and me Da at me back
To try for to win the Dog Derby via
The best of ould Ireland and Master McGrath.

They looked at me dog from in front and behind
They looked at me dog till I thought they was blind
The toffs in the stand gave a haughty 'Haw-haw'
'Is that the ould poodle to bate the McGrath.'

Me Da took a leap landed right in the stand
And he told'em me dog was the best in the land
At the top of his voice scrached me dacent oul'Da
'He'd bate the whole wurrild and Master McGrath'.

Me dog was took off and shut up in a box
With a wire thing in front like you'd put round a fox
The rabbit came out and he ran round and round
But the divil of a trace of me dog could be found.

For he was still locked up inside of that box
But when he came out shure 'twas then was the shocks
For out came me dog and caught up on the Hare
And ate up that cracher with nothing left spare

Now tho' up to then, me poor dog had been slow
'Twas then he proceeded to show 'em how to go
He was full of electric current you see –
For the rabbit was made be the ould E.S.B.

Comin' on to the bend he passed Master McGrath
'He's out on the road' sez me dacent ould Da
He passed out Prince Regent & Hyde on the straight
Comin' up to the signpost he passed a V. 8.

He passed out a Dodge and a Hillman Minx Ten
And then he turned round and he passed 'em again
Comin' into Mallow he passed out the train
Then he flew round Rineanna and came back again.

The Judges were spachless and looking at him yet
And they said 'Shure that dog must be run on a jet'
So they gave him the prize and I simply said 'Haw –
'How's that for ould Ireland and Master McGrath.'

Prince Regent, a famous racehorse, was winning all around him at
the time, and his jockey, Tim Hyde was equally winning fame.

18. THE SINKING OF THE MUIRCHU

Apart from 'The Bug-a-Boo', 'The 13th Lock', 'The Holy Ground' and 'The Irish Rover' (Like 'The Holy Ground' not really Irish in flavour) there are few enough Irish ballads about the sea.

One hopes, therefore, to be excused for giving in to the vanity of including one other of the ballads which I have myself churned out over the years. This was also written for a broadcast in a 'Cork Melodymakers' programme on May 16th. 1947, and commemorated the 'demise' of Ireland's 'battleship' at the time.

The Muirchu, an ex-British gunboat, served as the bulwark of the Republic's Navy for several years, and with some M.T.B.'s was the sole guardian of our shores for the war years.

As such she was an affectionate joke amongst the populace.

Shortly before the above mentioned date she was consigned to the scrap yard at Hammond Lane, Dublin, and set out from the anchorage at Haulbowline on her last journey. In true Naval tradition she defeated the hammer, and sank off the coast.

THE SINKING OF THE MUIRCHU
Words: James N. Healy
Air: The Boys of Wexford

She was a rare and fair boat
She was a fair and rare boat
She was a bliddy quare boat
The good old Muirchu.
I boarded her in Haul-bowline
With me lifeboat in me hand
All for the cause of freedom
And me dear ould native Land.
We joined the Muirchu me boys
To fight thro' shot and shell –
We got half-shot in Cobh, me boys
To brave the ocean's swell.

We started out for Dublin Town
The Captain steered us straight
But when we reached the ocean
The poor oul' ship was bate
She took one look at the rolling sea
And knew she could not do
So off the coast of Wexford
We lost the Muirchu.
We lost the Muirchu, me boys
Tho' she sailed with might and main
From Haul-bowline to Dublin Town
For scrap at Hammond Lane.

The Muirchu got lost at sea
Tho we searched everywhere
And when we turned and swam for shore
We could not find her there
But she'll live in song and story
The greatest ship of all
The guardian of our harbours
The Flagship of the Dàil

The good old Muirchu, me boys
Will never be a slave
For off the coast of Wexford
She found a sailors grave.

Before leaving maritime subjects I would particularly have liked
to include an emigrant ballad called 'Stop the Boat Let me out
and I'll walk' which an American relative of mine, one of the
Ward Sisters, used to sing on Broadway, but I have not been able
to get the words. It is about the crowded conditions, and other
unpleasant surroundings on an Irish emigrant ship bound for the
States, and like many of these Irish ballads makes fun of what was
in reality a rather grim situation, for the crowded and squalid
conditions on these emigrant ships in the period following the

famine of 1846/7, when the peasantry began to flee the country in thousands, was sometimes too horrible to describe, except by way of a grim joke.

Although from an American source it was undoubtedly inspired by someone who had the rather unpleasant experience somewhere in mid- or late-nineteenth century.

Ella Ward was originally one of the Longfield family, related to my grandmother, and her father had left for America around the 'eighties. As an old woman she paid an emigrant's visit to Ireland in the late 'twenties, and I, a very little boy, vaguely remember her blonde head seated at the piano while trying to pretend that I wasn't falling asleep so that I wouldn't be put to bed. She sang many songs, but I remember that one only and 'Shake Hands with your uncle Mike', which I believe she and her sister first brought out, and which subsequently became popular in Ireland about twenty years ago, under the name of 'Dear old Donegal'.

19. THE GROVES OF THE 'POOL
(De Groves ov de Pool)

I often heard my grandfather refer to this song which, despite the anti-rebel tendency of some of the verses, was a popular one in the Blackpool district up to the middle and latter parts of the last century.

There were, apparently, later variations, but the following is the original version, somewhat shortened, attributed to Dick Millikin and composed just after the suppression of the rising in 1798, when some of the Cork detachments of Militia had been used against the rebels in County Wexford. It is mainly notable for its humour, but also is an interesting sidelight on the confusion of the times sofaras, despite the United Irishmen's effort to organise the rising on a nation wide basis, Irish detachments which fought against the rebels would be greeted home as heroes (as by many they were) and that 'De Groves) would become a popular song (which it did).

By: R. A. Millikin

Now de war, dearest Nancy, is ended,
And the peace is come over from France,
So our gallant Cork city militia
Back again to headquarters advance.
No longer a beatin' dose rebels,
We'll now be a beatin' de bull,
And all oder genteel recreations
Dat are found in de Groves ov de Pool.
Chorus:
Ri fol de rol didder ol loddy, etc.

Wisha! ould Blackpool, 'tis I was longin to see you, says Jerry
Brophy, wipin the sweat off ov his forehead wid de tail ov his
wig – 'tis many a long march I had since I last tuck a look up
Dublin Hill. Oh, mudder! says Jerry to poor ould Mrs. Brophy,
you may thank Curnel Dawly over dere, for ever seein me alive;
bejekeys, you see at the battle ov Wexford, when de pike men
charged us, he ran away fust and we folly'd him.
Wid our ri fol didder rol, etc.

Den out came our lovin' relations
To see wor we livin' or no,
Besides all de jolly ould neighbours
All around us who flock'd in a row.
De noggins of sweet Tommy Walker
We lifted accordin' to rule,
And wetted our necks wid de native
Dats brewed in de Groves ov de Pool.
Chorus:
Ri fol de rol, etc.

Arrah! be de hokey, de girls ov Cork bates out all Ireland entirely for blood, bone, an beauty, says Corporal O'Mullighan. See how dey're oullin de ribbons out ov dere bonnets wid joy to see us safe an sound. Search de world all over, an who can hould a farden candle to um, fat an lean, long or short?
Wid dere ri fol didder rol etc.

> When de reg'ment marched into de Commons,
> 'Twould do your heart good for to see,
> You'd tink not a man nor a woman
> Was left in Cork's famous city;
> De boys dey came flockin' around us,
> Not a hat or wig stuck to a skull,
> All to compliment dose Irish heroes
> Dat sprung from 'de Groves ov de Pool.'
> *Chorus:*
> Ri fol de rol, etc.

Arrah! poor ould New Bridge, does I see you once more? says Paddy Kinnealy, blowin his nose. Yes, den, Bill, don't you remimber when dis bridge was a ferry, an all de ships would be walkin up an down by dereselves, your sowl to glory?
Wid your fol didder rol, etc.

> O! sure dere's no nation in Munster
> Wid de Groves ov de Pool can compare,
> Where dose heroes were all edicated,
> An de nymphs are so comely an' fair,
> Wid de gardens around entertainin'
> Wid sweet purty posies so full,
> Dat is worn by dose comely young creatures
> Dat walks in de 'Groves ov de Pool.'
> *Chorus:*
> Ri fol de rol, etc.

Arrah! where would you find sich a spot in de universal world for nature in all its beauty? Don't be botherin me about Greeshun an Roman heroes of ould, wid dere Romulus an Remus, an Pluto an Hector, an de rest of um. Don't be telling me about Venus, an Juno, an' Homer, and de likes in ould times. Show me among um all sich a daisy-cutter as Nelly Molloy over dere; or sich an ankel as Peg Deloohery can sport ov a fair day.
Wid her fol der didder rol, etc.

> Come all ye young youghts ov dis nation,
> Come fill up a bumper all round,
> Drink success to Blackpool navigation,
> And may it wid plenty be crown'd.
> Here's success to de jolly hoop-coilers,
> Likewise to de shuttle an spool;
> To de skinners, an worthy glue-boilers
> Dat lives in 'de Groves ov de Pool.'
> *Chorus:*
> Ri fol de rol, etc.

Well, well, says Larry Doolan, dey may talk ov 'de music ov de speres,' but to my taste, dere's notin to aiquil de hummin ov de shuttel an loom, dat's barrin only whin on Sunday evenin de boys and girls would be all in dere bibs and tuckers dancin at 'de Glory ov de World's' and listenin to Thady M'Kewin strikin up a strounkaun on de pipes, ov de ould ancient tune, describin de praises an recreashuns ov de beautiful 'Groves.'

The humour and the accent, as reproduced phonetically from the original, are both typically 'Cork', and might be heard in the Blackpool district today.

To speak of the 'sing-song Cork accent' however is to speak of a variety of accents – for one the rounded rather mealy-mouthed drawling accent of Montenotte and the professional classes. So 'Will you be arriving at the party on Saturday? Will

Gerald be there – he's great gas!' becomes with the stresses dropped in tone, and a cadence at the end of the sentence. –

– 'Will $_{yoo}$ be ur$_{riv}$ing et thu $_{por}$tee un $_{Sah}$ur ^{deh} Will $_{Jurrld}$

– be ^{thaare} He's $_{graat}$ $_{gaazz}$

This variation, now inherited, probably originally resulted from a deliberate attempt to copy the tones of the invaders social set; although there may be undertones in it of the Scandanavian origin of the merchants whose families ruled the City for so long. It comes from more or less the back of the throat, with a mouth pursed and only partly opened. The corresponding accent in Dublin is, rightly or wrongly, referred to as 'Rathmines'.

There is another Cork accent, flat, shrill, harsh and somewhat gutteral originating from what was formerly known as the Marsh area (the central part of the City enclosed roughly between the Opera House, St.Peter & Pauls Church and the Coal Quay) bearing influences of the Huguenot settlers, craftsmen and tradesmen who settled in, and indeed dominated, that area about two and a half centuries ago and began to use English at about the same time as it began to be used generally by the Irish-speaking population. So 'Bridget, come in out of that or I'll beat you' is transformed into: –

– Bri^{jit} cumm-$_{in}$-our-$_{raht}$-orr I'll $_{bate}$ cha

Anyone unused to this particular variation would probably need an interpreter on the Coal Quay on a market morning.

The most generally heard accent, a softer lower-middle class one is an uneasy mixture of these two with various graduations up and down the social and musical scale. To find what could be classed as the real Cork accent amongst all these would be difficult enough, but the purest is probably that heard in Blackpool, reproduced by Millikin in 'The Groves'. This is somewhat nasal, and often spoken out of the side of the mouth when confidential emphasis is required (as in the nature of the City it often is)

6 – Cumm *mere* to me *bhaw*ev – howse yer *ole* wang'yeame ba^{wl}

(Come here to me, boy – hows your old one (mother) – game ball?

This is a fascinating accent, with wonderful turns of phrase, and can be regarded as the purest in that it has probably come directly from the native Irish who clustered and settled around the North Gate Bridge, being denied residence in the city itself over many years. The settlement gradually spread northwards and developed industries such as, tanning, brewing and spinning enveloping the 'Groves of Blackpool', of which the poet sings.

The accent today differs little from its phonetic reproduction by Millikin a hundred and sixty years ago. Will it be the same a hundred and sixty years from now? One doubts it. Apart from the generally levelling influences of radio and films on localised dialects, families, with greater travel facilities and housing extensions tend to move from settled districts now more than before: from city to city, and even within districts of a city. Expanding new districts have sprung up in Cork at Gurrane-braher, Spangle Hill, Ballyphehane for instance, which have absorbed former inhabitants of the Marsh and other areas with a resultant dispersal of areas where a particular local dialect held sway, and an admixture in these new areas.

Overtones of the old dialects will undoubtedly remain, but will tend to be less pronounced as the years go on. The Cork City accent, in its various forms, is very localised, and it disappears within a mile of the City limits.

Some explanatory notes to this ballad may not be out of place.

Verse 1 The 'war' referred to is that already mentioned – the United Irishmen rising of 1798 which so gallantly failed at Wexford.

'Peace from France' refers to the impending defeat of Napoleon. 'Beating the Bull' – Bull baiting, one of the illegal 'sports' of the time: maybe also a sly dig at John Bull. Dublin Hill – an eminence overlooking Blackpool, now a built up area.

Verse 2 'Tommy Walker' – product of a now defunct distillery. 'De native' – Porter or Stout, probably Arnotts.

Murphys, who now brew stout in the locality, did not take over Lady's Well Brewery until 1857: until then it had been an orphanage, referred to in one of the verses omitted.

Verse 3 'De Commons' – the Commons Road, the main entry into Blackpool from the City. The 'New Bridge' probably refers to Patricks Bridge, although different bridges over the Lee have been referred to as the 'new' bridge from time to time.

Verse 5 'Hoop Coilers' – Coopers: 'Shuttle and Spool' – the weaving trade: 'Skinners and glue boilers' – Tannery and subsiduary trades.

'Strounkaun' – wailing

20. BEN THE COACHMAN

Words: J. N. Healy senior
Music: J. N. Healy senior

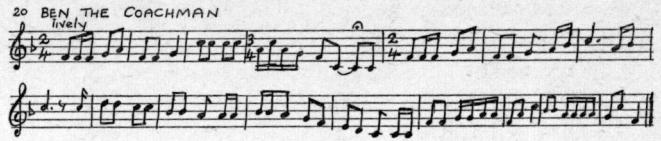

Ben was a Hackney coachman rare,
(Jarveys, Jarveys, Jerry-mac-a-rogner.)*
And loudly he'd curse and loudly swear,
(Timmy – roo, Timmy roo.)*
A handsome cabby he did drive,
And his number-a hundred and sixty-five,
(With a ran-tan-tivvy-tivvy-tivy-O
ran-tan-tivvy-tivvy-tivy-O.)*

As Ben was driving out one day
(Jarveys, etc.)
A handsome gent came by his way
(Timmy – roo, etc.)
'Come here my man, for I would drive,
With your number-a hundred and sixty-five'
(With a ran-tan-tivvy, etc.)

He held a book in his left claw
Just for to show that he studied the law
But 'tho he appeared to be mighty civil
Ben knew very well that he was the Divil.

Says Ben to the Divil 'Where will I go?'
As if the old fool did'nt know
The Divil thought he'd cut a swell
So he said to Ben 'drive straight to Hell'.

* each verse.

So Ben jumped up and he drove pell-mell
Until he arrived at the gates of Hell
And when he arrived at the Gates of Sin
Sure he turned around and he backed the Divil in.

Says the Divil to Ben what is your fare
'Why Twenty Guineas for driving you here'
The Divil paid without a grin,
For the thought that he'd get old Ben in.

Says the Divil to Ben 'Your coach I'll burn'
When Ben jumped up fast to return
'The horse and coach may go to pot
For they're insured but I am not'.

So Ben jumped up and drove off fast
Until he arrived safe home at last
Now Ben doesn't curse, nor does he swear
Nor for the Divil does he care,
(With a Ran-tan-tivvy, etc.).

BEN THE COACHMAN

This was the one I most clearly remember my grandfather singing, and it is the only special one of his, besides the 'Bug-a-Boo' and 'The Goat' of which I can get the words.

The only other song I know like it, where a man has a mental and verbal contest with 'The Devil' is that song of the North called 'Killyburn Brae', which for sake of comparison I am following with.

Words: traditional
Air: traditional

They say that the women is wors'n the men,
(Right full, right ful, tit-ee-full-ay)
They say that the women is wors'n the men
When they go down to hell, they are threw out again.
(Singin' right-fol-lol: titty-fol-lol
right-fol-lol: right-fol-de-di-day)
(*for the remainder we will quote lines three and four of each verse
only, as the reader can fill in the 'titty-fol-lols' himself*)

There was an oul' man of Killyburn Brae
Had a scoldin' oul' wife for the most of his day

One day as this man he walked out in the Glen
He met with the Divil sayin' 'How are you, then'

Sez he 'Me oul' man, I have come for your wife
For I hear she's the plague and torment of your life.'

So the Divil he h'isted her up on his back
And he hustled for hell with her tied in a sack.

And when at the finish they got to hell's gate
He threw her right down with a bump on her pate.

There were two little Divils, a-tied up with chains
She up with her stick and she scattered their brains.

There were four little Divils, a-playin' handball
She up with her stick, an' she scattered them all.

So the Divil he h'isted her up on his back
They were seven years going, nine days coming back.

Sez he, 'Me oul' man, here's your wife safe and well,
For the likes of herself we would not have in hell'.

So it's true that the women is wors'n the men
When they go down to hell, they are threw out again.

I am including this in 'The Family Circle' section because I first heard it from the mother of one of my greatest friends – Mrs Fanny Dwyer of Mayfield House – at parties when we were young lads together. She was originally a Scroope from Galway and brought the song from that county with her.

It is an old country song – probably dating from about or before 1860, the time of informers, Fenians and the 'soljering' at Kabul.

For the sake of brevity the 4th and 6th verses could be omitted when it is being sung.

ME DARLIN' OULD STICK

Words: traditional
Air: 'Teddy O'Toole'

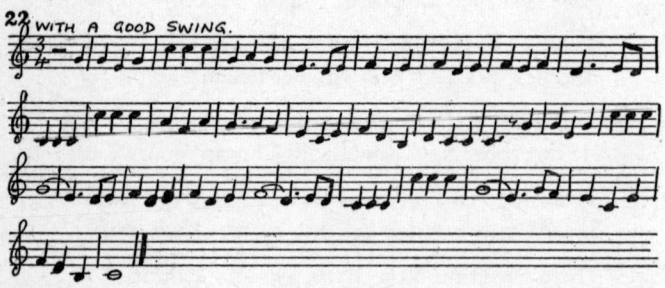

My name is Morgan M'Carthy, from Trim,
My relations is dead barrin wan brother, Jim,
And he's gone a soljering out to Cowbull,
Maybe he's laid low with a puck in the skull;
But let him be dead or be living,
A prayer for his corpse I'll be giving,
To send him soon home, or to heaven,
For he left me this bit of a stick.

If that stick had a tongue it could tell you some tales,
How it battered the countenance of the O'Neills,
It made bits of skull fly about in the air,
And it's been the promoter of fun at each fair;
And I swear be the toenails of Moses,
It often broke bridges of noses
Of the faction that dared to oppose us,
It's the darlin' kippeen of a stick.

The last time it was used was on Patrick's day,
When Larry Fegan and I got into a fray.
We went to a fair by the town of Athboy,
Where we danced, and, when done, I kiss'd Kate M'Evoy;
Then her sweetheart went out for his cousin,
And bejabers, he brought in a dozen,
And a Doldrum they would have had us in,
If I hadn't my bit of a stick.

'War!' was the word when the faction came in,
And to pummel us well they peeled off to the skin;
Like a Hercules there I stood for the attack,
And the first that came up I sent down on his back;
Then I shoved out the eye of Pat Clancy,
For he once floored me dear sister Nancy,
In the meantime poor Kate took a fancy
To myself and my bit of a stick.

I smathered her sweetheart until he was black,
She then tipped me the wink – we were off in a crack.
We went to a house t'other end of the town,
Where we kept up our spirits by letting some down;
When I got her snug into a corner,
And the whisky beginning to warm her,
She said, 'My sweetheart's an informer,'
Oh! 'twas then I said prayers for my stick.

We got whiskificated to such a degree,
For support my poor Kate had to sit on my knee;
I promised to see her safe to her abode,
But soon, faith, we fell in the mud in the road.
We were roused by the magistrate's order,
Before we could get a toe further,
Surrounded by peelers for murther
Was myself and my innocent stick.

When the trial came on Katty swore to the fact,
That before I set-to I was decently whacked,
And the judge, who'd a little more feeling than sense,
Said that what I had done was but in self-defence,
But one chap swore agin me, named Carey,
Though that night he was in Tipperary,
He'd swear a coal porter was a canary,
To transport myself and my stick.

When I was acquitted I leap'd from the dock,
And then all my comrades soon around me did flock,
I'd a pain in my shoulder, I shook hands so often,
For the boys all imagined I'd see my own coffin;
I went and bought a gold ring, boys,
And Kate to the priest I did bring, boys.
So next night you come, I will sing, boys –
The adventures of me and my stick.

It wouldn't be too difficult to fill an entire book with versions of the 'Toor-al-i-ay' tune, although it mightn't be the best way of completing a ballad book. Another Waterford variation which my grandfather had, rarely if ever heard now, is 'The Goat', in which the tune is slightly varied. This came from the West Waterford side, and probably predates the Master McGrath number by some twenty years.

It is the earliest song I ever remember, as apparently, for some peculiar reason it was used at home as a song to get me to sleep. Since, from the age of 1 ½ to 2, I usually joined in it was abandoned for this purpose, and no wonder.

THE GOAT

Words: traditional
Music: arr. James N. Healy

When I was a lad, about 10 years or more
I lived in a place near the town of Tramore
Me father he came from a place called Ardmore
He kep' a cow and a calf and a nate Billy goat.

Now this same goat had a most peculiar way
He'd go out in the morning and stop out all day
And when he'd come in like a bull he would roar.
Till me poor father got up and let him in be the door.

One day at dinner we all sat down to ate
The goat jumped on the table and ate all the mate
And when he was done like a baste of a grummock
He stuck his two horns in me fathers poor stomach.

'Arrah Jim', says me mother, 'what's that ma'am' says I
'Take the goat to the market and sell him, do try'
The words were scarce spoke when the goat gave a jump
And hit me poor mother a bump in the rump.

Not long after that we all beat a retreat
For the goat pucked away at the divil's own rate
And when we looked in through a split in the door
He was pucking the dishes all over the floor.

From the table he jumped to a coat in the hall.
He pucked away at the tails till he put his head through the wall
And all that was found on the very next day,
Was the stump of his tail and it puckin' away.

The one which follows is another variant of 'Toor-al-i-ay';
from the North this time where (as in the Widow of Donaghadee)
it is a frequently used tune.

THE OULD ORANGE FLUTE

Words: Nugent Bohem
Air: 'Toor-al-i-ay'

In the County Tyrone near the town of Dungannon,
Where mony a ruction myself had a han'in,
Bob Williamson lived, a weaver to trade,
And each of us thought him a stout orange blade.
On the twelfth of July, as it yearly did come,
Bob played on the flute, and we banged on the drum,
Ye may talk of your harp, yer piano, or lute,
But there's nothing can sound like the ould orange flute.

Chorus:
Toor-al-oo; Toor-al-ay, singing Toor-al-i-toor-al-i-
Toor-al-i-ay

But this treacherous scoundrel, he took us all in,
For he married a Popish named Bridget McGinn,
Turned Popish himself and forsook the oul' cause
That gave us our freedom, religion and laws,
The boys in the townland made some noise upon it,
And Bob had to fly to the Province of Connaught;
He fled with his wife, and his fixings to boot,
And along with all others the ould orange flute.

At Mass every Sunday to atone for his past deeds,
He said Paters and Aves and counted his glass beads,
Till after some time, at the Priest's own desire,
He went with his ould flute to play in the choir.
He went with his ould flute to play in the Mass,
And the instrument shivered and sighed, 'Oh, alas'
As he blew it and fingered it made a strange noise,
For the flute would play only 'The Protestant Boys.'

Bob started and jumped and he got in a splutter,
And he threw his ould flute in the blessed holy water,
For he thought that this charm would bring some other sound,
When he played it again, it played 'Croppies lie down',
And all he could whistle and finger and blow
To play Popish music, he found it no go;
'Kick the Pope' and 'Boyne Water' and such like 'twould sound,
But one Popish squeak in it could not be found.

At the Council of Priests which was held the next day,
They decided to banish the ould flute away,
For they couldn't knock heresy out of its head,
So they bought Bob another to play in its stead.
So the flute was condemned and its fate was pathetic,
It was fastened and burned at the stake as heretic,
As the flames rose around it they heard a strange noise,
'Twas the ould flute still whistling 'The Protestant Boys.'

I particularly like The Ould Orange Flute; perhaps because I have
known it a long time, but more so because I have heard both
Protestants and Catholics singing it at various times and both
getting fun out of it: in its apparent rancour there is no ill-feeling
and great good-humour, and surely that is how we would all
wish it to be. The clipped Northern accent is almost essential for
an effective and authentic performance of the song.

25. NED FLAHERTY'S DRAKE

Words: traditional
Music: 'Ned Flaherty's Drake'
arr James N. Healy

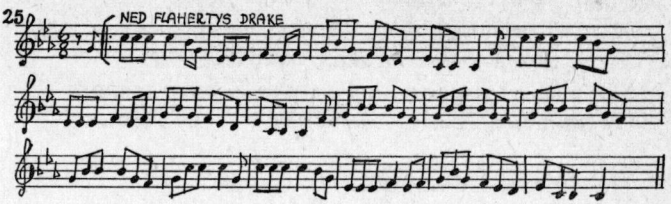

Me name it is Ned, and 'tis candidly said
That I live near Cork City, which I won't deny.
I had a fine drake, sure I'd die for its sake,
That me gran'mother left and she going to die.
The dear little fella, his legs they were yella,
The universe round I would rove for his sake,
But some dirty savage to grease his white cabbage
Has murdered Ned Flaherty's beautiful drake.

May his pig never grunt, may his cat never hunt,
May a ghost ever haunt him at dead of the night,
May his hen never lay, may his ass never bray,
May his goat fly away like an old paper kite,
That the flies and the fleas may the wretch ever tease,
May the biting north breeze make him shiver and shake,
Bad wind to the robber be he drunk or sober,
That murdered Ned Flaherty's beautiful drake.

May his pipe never smoke, may his tay-pot be broke
And to add to the joke may his kittle ne'er boil,
May he stick to the bed till the hour that he's dead,
May he always be fed on hogswash and boiled oil
May he swell with the gout, may his grinders fall out,
May he roll, howl and shout with the horrid toothache,
May his temples wear horns, and the toes many corns
Of the monster that murdered Ned Flaherty's drake.

May his dog yelp and howl, with the hunger and cold,
May his wife ever scold till his hair it turns grey,
May the curse of each hag that e'er carried a bag,
Alight on his head 'till his hair it turns grey,
May witches affright him, that mad dogs may bite him,
And everyone slight him asleep or awake,
May plague take the scamp, that the divil may stamp
On the monster that murdered Ned Flaherty's drake.

The only good news that I have to infuse,
Is that old Paddy Hughes and Blind Peter McCrake,
And Big-nosed Bob Manson and Buck-toothed Ned Hanson,
Each man have a grandson of my darlin' drake,
Me treasure had dozens of nephews and cousins,
And one I must get or me heart it will break,
To make me mind aisy, or else I'll run crazy,
That ends the whole song of Ned Flaherty's drake.

I suppose everyone has a favourite ballad, and depending on the
number of times one sings a song, 'The Drake, is mine.

This is the version I find best for singing. There are a great
number of verses, some of which have probably been added by
different hands, but it is best not to make it too long. In the
middle (cursing) verses it is particularly important when singing
it to keep a good driving pace, although the first half of the first
and last verses can be slowed down to lend additional emphasis.
I have heard the whole thing sung slowly once or twice and it can
be dreary beyond measure. This was an old ballad at the turn of
the century, and probably dates in its original form, from mid-
nineteenth century days, when a great number of ballads of this
type were being written.

I first picked it up in West Cork during the thirties, when I
used to spend holidays there, and gradually pieced the words together, and got the correct tune from a very old dance music
copy: but the ballad originally may have come from the Midlands of the North where it is sometimes known as 'Nell Fla-

herty's Drake', and, in places in-correctly sung to a variant of 'Toor-al-i-ay'.

For the record here are additional verses which some readers may prefer to substitute for those I have quoted above.

His neck it was green – most rare to be seen,
He was fit for a queen of the highest degree;
His body was white, and would you delight,
He was plump, fat and heavy, and brisk as a bee,
The dear little fellow, his legs they were yellow
He would fly like a swallow and dive like a hake,
But some wicked savage to grease his white cabbage
Has murdered Nell Flaherty's beautiful drake.

May his cradle ne'er rock, may his box have no lock
May his wife have no frock to cover her back
May his cock never crow, may his bellows ne'er blow,
And his pipe and his pot may he evermore lack.
May his duck never quack, may his goose it turn black
And pull down his turf with her long yellow beak.
May weasels still gnaw him; and jackdaws still claw him
The monster that murdered Nell Flaherty's drake.

May his spade never dig, may his sow never pig,
May each hair in his wig be well thrashed with a flail;
May his door have no latch, may his house have no thatch
May his turkey not hatch, may the rats eat his meal.
May every old fairy, from Cork to Dunleary,
Dip him snug and airy in river or lake,
Where the eel and the trout may feed on the snout
Of the monster that murdered Nell Flaherty's drake

Ballads of Munster

The different counties of Munster, apart from Cork, are prolific in Balladry, some of them in the preceding pages, where they have been included as tie-up references with other songs; and also, some of those in the 'Family Circle' are from parts of Munster other than Cork. In the pages following are some from each county – Clare, Kerry, Limerick, and Tipperary. 'The Goat' on page 67 is from Waterford.

Clare

26. KATE OF GARNAVILLA

Edward Lysaght was a native of Clare, where he was born in 1763, and his gay nature won him the nickname of 'Pleasant Ned.' He was quite a productive song-writer, and this song, now neglected, was very popular in its time. He died in 1810.

The tune is one of many which is claimed by both Scotland and Ireland; which is a sufficient indication of its antiquity. Burns wrote a song to the same air called 'Canst thou leave me thus, my Katy', and Gerald Griffin (Author of 'The Collegians') wrote a version which is lyrically superior to Lysaghts set of verses, but far inferior as a singing medium to the lively air.

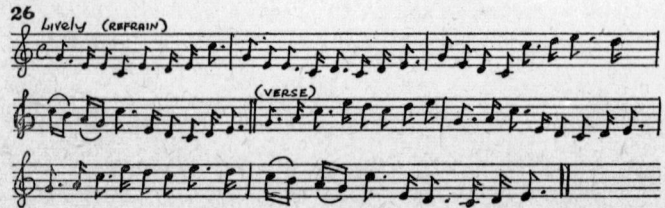

KATE OF GARNAVILLA

Words: Edward Lysaght
Air: 'Roy's wife of Aldivalloch

Have you been at Garnavilla?
Have you seen at Garnavilla
Beauty's train trip o'er the plain
With lovely Kate of Garnavilla?
Oh! She's pure as virgin snows
Ere they light on woodland hill; O
Sweet as dew-drop on wild rose
Is lovely Kate of Garnavilla!

Philomel, I've listened oft
To thy lay, nigh weeping willow;
Oh, the strain's more sweet, more soft,
That flows from Kate of Garnavilla!
Have you been, &c.
As a noble ship I've seen
Sailing o'er the swelling billow,
So I've marked the graceful mien
Of lovely Kate of Garnavilla.
Have you been, &c.

If poets' prayers can banish cares,
No cares shall come to Garnavilla;
Joy's bright rays shall gild her days,
And dove-like peace perch on her pillow.
Charming maid of Garnavilla!
Lovely maid of Garnavilla!
Beauty, grace, and virtue wait
On lovely Kate of Garnavilla!

Kerry

27. THE ROSE OF TRALEE

The story of young John Mulchinock and his unhappy romance with Mary O'Connor, the Rose of Tralee, has passed to the legendary of the Kerry Town, where his song has become so loved that a monument to him, and it, has been erected in the Town Park. Mulchinock's house is situated on a narrow road running through Clahane (the first turn right after the barracks coming from the town) and the song comes to life amazingly as you stand there, – the mountains to the far off right; in front of you the vale of Tralee. The situation of the 'pure crystal fountain' has been disputed, but it is almost certainly the river Lee, which gives its name to the town, and which cuts across the townland to the left looking from Mulchinock's house. 'The Rose' is said to have been a servant in the house; his parents sent him abroad in order to keep them apart; Mary had died of consumption on his return but he never forgot her, and wrote the song late in life when he was blind and lonely.

THE ROSE OF TRALEE
Words and Music: John Mulchinock

The pale moon was rising above the green mountain,
The sun was declining beneath the blue sea,
When I strayed with my love to the pure crystal fountain
That stands in the beautiful vale of Tralee.
She was lovely and fair as the rose of summer,
Yet 'twas not her beauty alone that won me.
Oh, no! 'twas the truth in her eyes ever dawning
That made me love Mary,
The Rose of Tralee.

The cool shades of evening their mantle were spreading,
And Mary all smiling was list'ning to me.
The moon thro' the valley her pale rays was shedding,
When I won the heart of the Rose of Tralee.
Though lovely and fair as the rose of summer,
Yet 'twas not her beauty alone that won me,
Oh, no! 'twas the truth in her eyes ever dawning,
That made me love Mary,
The Rose of Tralee.

28. THE KERRY RECRUIT

This earthy ballad dates from the middle part of the 19th century
when the recruiting sergeant was at the height of his rather
dreaded powers. I have referred to this gentry in an extended
note to the ballad 'The Widow McGrath' later on in the book,
and it suffices to say when speaking of the Kerry Recruit that it is
certainly a spirited affair which well expresses the 'live-for-today'
attitude of the farming community of the time, even under the
difficult circumstances in which they had to exist and the
fondness, one might even say the habit, of wishing to go abroad
and see places even at the expense of a limb. This must be rendered broadly, with a spirit of not caring for God nor man; or
even recruiting sergeants.

Words and Music: Traditional

One morning in March I was digging the land,
With a pair of ould brouges and a spade in me hand.
When up came a sergeant and axed me to list,
'Yerra, sergeant', says I 'stick a bob in me fist'.
With me Kerry – I – Oh – Whack fol di dol day
Kerry – I – Oh – Whack fol di dol day.

'Here is a shilling, I've got no more,
When you go to headquarters, you dare get a score.'
'Head quarters' says I, 'A gra, sergeant, good-bye,
You wouldn't like to be quartered and neither would I.'
With me Kerry – I – Oh – Whack fol di dol day
Kerry – I – Oh – Whack fol di dol day.

The first thing they gave me it was a red coat,
With a white strap of leather to tie round me throat.
They gave me a queer thing – I axed 'em 'What's that?'
They told me it was a cockade for me hat.
With me Kerry – I – Oh – Whack fol di dol day
Kerry – I – Oh – Whack fol di dol day.

The next thing they gave me it was a big gun,
Right down on the trigger they placed me big thumb.
Yerra first she spit fire and then she spit smoke,
And she gave me ould shoulder the hell of a stroke.
With me Kerry – I – Oh – Whack fol di dol day
Kerry – I – Oh – Whack fol di dol day.

The next thing they gave me it was a grey horse,
With bridle and saddle and two legs across.
When gave me bould charger a prick of the steel
Yerra, cushla ma chree, sure she up with her heel.
With me Kerry – I – Oh – Whack fol di dol day
Kerry – I – Oh – Whack fol di dol day.

The next place they sent me was down to the quay,
On board a big ship that was bound for Crimea.
Three sticks in the middle all covered with sheet
And she walked in the waters without any feet.
With me Kerry – I – Oh – Whack fol di dol day
Kerry – I – Oh – Whack fol di dol day.

Then up came the sergeant a man of great fame,
He axed me me country, I told him my name,
I told him before and I'll tell him again,
That me father and mother were two Kerry men.
With me Kerry – I – Oh – Whack fol di dol day
Kerry – I – Oh – Whack fol di dol day.

Now five years are up and I'm glad tisn't ten:
I'll go home to Tralee and dig praties again,
I'll butter me brogues and shake hands with me spade.
For I find that this fighting's a bloody bad trade.
With me Kerry – I – Oh – Whack fol di dol day
Kerry – I – Oh – Whack fol di dol day.

29. THE SIVE SONG

Here is a song, written within the last five years, which has the
true spirit of the Irish ballad. Why should only traditional
ballads be included in collections? – all ballads were originally
written by someone, even tho' the authors of many of the best
from the 19th century have never been recorded: but, above all,
ballads were made to be sung. John B's ballad from the play Sive
swept the country when it was first heard in 1959. In addition the
lyric has real literary quality. This is the longer version; which
Keane wrote specially; not all the words are used in the play.
Keane has a great ear and love for the ballad, and it is to be hoped
that there will be more from him in the years to come.

Words: John B. Keane
Music: arr. James N. Healy to traditional tune
(published by Pigott & Co.)

To be sung
Oh, come all good men and true, a sad tale I'll tell to you
Of the maiden who was known to me as Sive
She was young and sweet and fair but that household sad and bare
Her marriage to an old man would contrive.

To be recited
Now the Tinkers son came in to that house of want and sin
And his father Pats Bocock smote on the floor
Saying 'Carthalawn, my blade, let a noble song be made
Bringing plenty on this house for evermore'

To be sung
'Oh, Mike Glavin, you're the man; you was always in the van
With an open door to oul' man and gorsoon
May white snuff be at your wake, bakers bread and currany cake
And the plenty on your table late and soon.'

To be recited
But they scorned the Tinkers son when his song of praise was
And his father Pats Bocock smote on the floor   [done
Saying 'Carthalawn my jewel, let a song both wild and cruel
Settle down upon this house for evermore'

To be sung
'On the Road from Abbeyfeale, sure I met a man with meal
Come here says he and pass your idle time
On me he made quite bold, saying the young will wed the old
And the old man have the money for the child'

To be recited
Now Thomasheen Rua the liar, was sat down 'longside the fire
And he sold the girl Sive that very night
Pats Bocock made on his quest, saying 'sing your mighty best'
And the Song of Carthalawn was like a blight

To be sung
May the snails devour his corpse, and the rains do harm worse
May the devil sweep the hairy creature soon
He's as greedy as a sow; as a crow behind the plough
The black man from the mountain, Seaneen Rua
May his brains and eyeballs burst, may he screech with awful
That melted amadawn; that big bostoon   [thirst
May the fleas ate up his bed, and the mange consume his head
The black man from the mountain, Seaneen Rua
To be recited
But the bonny Sive took flight, like a wild bird in the night,
And the waters washed her small white body o'er
And her true love found her there, and he stacked her golden
And he laid her on the dark and dismal shore   [hair

Then outspoke bold Pats Bocock and his voice was sad with shock
And his face was grey as winter when he cried
He said 'Carthalawn, my gem, Let you make a woeful hymn
All of this day and of the one who died'
To be sung
'Oh, come all good men and true, a sad tale I'll tell to you
All of a maiden fair who died this day
Oh, they drownded lovely Sive, for she wouldn't be a bride
And they laid her dead to bury in the clay'

Limerick

30. THE CO. LIMERICK BUCK HUNT

This old hunting song was written by Pierce Creagh of Dangan,
in the Co. Limerick about 1735. The piece has no great literary
pretensions: like others of its time (and many which never
survived) it was probably written for a small gathering of inti-
mate friends of the Chase, to be sung while the 'bumpers passed
round' on a convivial occasion.

Creagh was a country gentleman and it is interesting to reflect how well he, and others of his class were acquainted with the native airs since this and so many of their compositions have survived. Some of the families mentioned such as that of the Miss Persse, towards whom Creagh shows so definite a leaning, are still living in the district. There were many hunting songs so written, another of the same style and period being 'The Kilruddery Hunt' by Thomas Mozeen which relates to the country around Dublin, and which is included later in the book.

THE COUNTY LIMERICK BUCK-HUNT

Words: Pierce Creagh
Air: Nac Mbaineann sin do

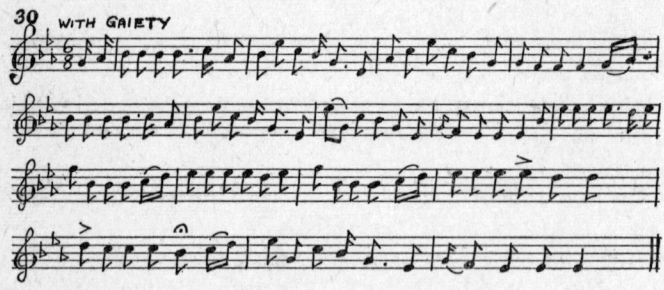

By your leave, Larry Grogan,
Enough has been spoken;
'Tis time to give over your sonnet, my boy!
Come listen to mine, 'Tis far better than thine
Though not half the time was spent on it, my boy!
'Tis of a buck slain
In this very campaign:
To let him live longer 'twere pity, my boy!
For fat and for haunches,
For head and for branches,
Exceeding the mayor of a city, my boy!

A council assembled
(Who'd think but he trembled)
Of lads of good spirit, well mounted, my boy!
Each with whip and with cap on,
And spurs made of Ripon,
A score, aye and more, sure we counted, my boy!
Off at once we went bounding,
Sweet horns were resounding,
Each youth filled the air with a halloa, my boy!
Dubourg, were he there
Such sweet music to hear,
Would leave his Cremona and follow, my boy!

Knockaderk and Knockaney,
And hills twice as many,
We flew their stone walls and their ditches, my boy!
The buck skimmed the grounds,
But to baffle our hounds
Was never in any buck's breeches, my boy!
Four hours he held out
Most surprisingly stout,
Till at length to his fate he submitted, my boy!
His throat being cut up,
The poor culprit put up,
 To the place where he came was remitted, my boy!

Then the bumpers went round,
With an elegant sound,
Chink, chink, like sweet bells went the glasses my boy!
We drank queen and king
And each other fine thing,
Then bumpered the beautiful lasses, my boy!
There was Singleton (Cherry),
And sweet Sally Curry,
Miss Croker, Miss Bligh, and Miss Prittie, my boy!
With lovely Miss Persse,
That subject for verse,
Who shall ne'er be forgot in my ditty, my boy!

31. PADDY HEGGARTY'S BREECHES

Like many of these old country ballads I find this one too long, and when singing it think it preferable to omit verses 2 and 6. Even then it is a little long, but it would be difficult to shorten it further without losing the sense of the narrative. At any rate keep it going at a well-marked waltz tempo, and you will find it rewarding singing.

PADDY HEGGARTY'S LEATHER BREECHES

Words and Music: traditional

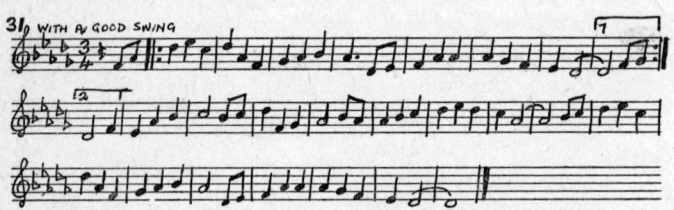

At the sign of the Bell, on the road to Clonmel,
Paddy Heggarty kept a neat Sheebeen,
Sold pigs'-meat and bread, kept a good lodging bed,
Was well liked in the country he lived in.
Himself and his wife, they struggled through life;
On the weekdays Pat mended the ditches,
But on Sundays he dressed in a coat of the best,
And his pride was his old leather breeches.

For twenty-one years, at least so it appears,
His father those breeches had run in;
The morning he died he to his bedside
Called Paddy, his own darling son in.
Advice then he gave ere he went to his grave,
For he could not boast of his riches,
Says he, "Tis no use to get into my shoes,
But I'd like you to leap in my breeches.'

Now last winter's snow left victuals so low,
That Paddy was ate out completely;
With the snow coming down, he could not get to town;
And the hunger did bother him greatly.
One night as he lay a-dreaming away
About ghosts, fairies, spirits and witches,
He heard an uproar just outside the door,
And he jumped up to pull on his breeches.

Says big Brian Burke, with a voice like a Turk,
'Come Paddy, and get us some ateing.'
Says big Andy Moore, 'We'll shove open the door,
Sure, this is no night to be waiting.'
The words were scare spoke when the door it was broke,
And they crowded round Paddy like leeches,
And the swore be the fates, if they didn't get ates,
They would ate him clane out of his breeches.

Poor Paddy in dread slipped up to the bed
That held Judy, his darling ould wife, in,
And there 'twas agreed that they should get a feed,
So he slipped out and brought a big knife in.
He ripped off the waist of his breeches, the baste,
And he pulled out the buttons and stiches;
He cut them in strips, just the way you would tripes,
And boiled down his oul leather breeches.

The tripes they stewed on a dish they were strewed,
And the boys all roared out, 'Lord be thank-ed.'
But Heggarty's wife was afraid of her life,
And she thought it high time to shank it.
To see how they smiled, for they thought Paddy boiled
Some mutton or beef of the richest.
But they little knew it was leather burgoo
That was made out of Paddy's old breeches.

As they looked on the stuff, says Darby, 'It's tough!'
Says Paddy, 'You're no judge of Mutton;'
When big Brian Burke, on the heel of his fork,
Held up a big ivory button,
Says Paddy, 'What's that? Sure, I thought it was fat;'
Brian leaps to his feet and he screeches,
'By the powers above, I was trying to shove
My teeth through the seat of his breeches.'

They all jumped at Pat, but he got out of that;
He ran when he saw them all rising
Says Brian, 'Make haste and go for the praste,
By the Holy Saint Patrick, I'm poisoned.'
Revenge for the joke they had, for they broke
All the chairs, tables, bottles, and dishes;
And ever since that night they'd knock out your daylight,
At the mention of old leather breeches.

32. SLIEVENAMON

The beautiful valley lying under Slievenamon near Clonmel in
Co. Tipperary has been commemorated using a sweet ballad
which is sung with great feeling in all the area around. This
mountainous, but extremely fertile district of South-East Tipperary is lovely to see, and rewarding to visit, with its pleasant
people. Charles Kickham from near Clonmel was a prolific
novel writer and poet of the last century, and his works, amongst
them Knocknagow (they seem a little wordy now) were very
popular some years ago.

Knocknagow was made into a musical only last year in Clonmel.

SLIEVENAMON

Words: Charles Kickham
Music: Traditional

Alone, all alone, by the wave-washed strand
All alone in the crowded hall,
The hall it is gay and the waves they are grand
But my heart is not there at all,
It flies far away, by night and by day
To the times and the joys that are gone
But I never can forget the sweet maiden I met
In the valley of Slievenamon.

It was not the grace of her queenly air
Nor the cheeks of the roses glow
Her soft dark eyes or her curly hair,
Nor was it her lily white brow.
'Twas the soul of truth and of melting ruth,
And a smile like the summer's day.
That stole my heart away on that bright summer's day
In the valley of sweet Slievenamon.

In the festive hall and the wave-washed shore
My restless spirit cries –
'My land, oh my land, shall I never see you more,
My country will you never uprise'.
By night and by day I will ever, ever pray,
As darkly my life it rolls on,
To see our flag unrolled and my true love unfold
In the valley near Slievenamon.

Words: John Ryan
Music: Traditional

There was a bold Tipperary boy,
From the Glens of Aherlow,
He sang the song of his country's wrong,
Where the lovely Anner flows,
And as he took me by the hand,
His happy home to leave,
Forced by England's treachery,
To fill a Rebel's grave.
Chorus:
Goodnight my honest neighbour,
I'll call to see you soon,
For tonight I'm on to Slievenamon
Where brightly shines the moon,
I'll seek the woods of sweet Glenbower,
Or in some rock or cave,
For glory and for Ireland's sake,
To fill a Rebel's grave.

For six long weary months he roamed
The rocky mountain side,
The heather for his pillow
And by his friends supplied,
And as he roamed, outlawed from home,
From rise 'till set of sun,
At night, he'd steal down wood and glen,
A Rebel on the run.

A traitor crept among us,
And the cause it soon was sold,
To the hirelings of the British Queen,
For the greedy Saxon gold.
But Fenian men will rise again,
Their country's soul to save,
And strike a blow for liberty,
And fill a Rebel's grave.

A British soldier caused his death,
By a riffle shot he fell,
The red-brown heath if it could speak,
His bravery would tell.
A Saxon soldier he laid low,
In the gallant fight he made,
And now he sleeps in old Kilcash,
And fills a Rebel's grave.

This ballad was written by John Ryan, a national teacher in Clonmel, who in his young days was a friend of Kickham and John O'Mahony, the Fenian leader of South Tipperary, who lived near Kilbeheny.

I got it from his son James Ryan one September day walking by the river in Clonmel when the Suir was in brown flood.

It was written after the rising at Ballingarry in 1867. The grave of the hero, Kelly, will be found at Kilcash.

There is another, later, ballad to Patrick Sheehan written to the same old air.

Words: Darby Ryan
Air: Traditional

As Bansha peelers were, one night, on duty a-patrolling, O,
They met a goat upon the road who seemed to be a-strolling, O
With bayonets fixed they sallied forth, and caught her by the
[wizen, O,
And then swore out a mighty oath they'd send her off to prison,
[O.

'O, mercy, sirs,' the goat replied; 'pray, let me tell my story, O;
I am no Rogue or Ribbonman, no Croppy, Whig or Tory, O.
I'm guilty not of any crime of petty or high treason, O,
And I'm sadly wanted at this time, for 'tis the milking season, O.'
Peeler:
'It is in vain you do complain, or give your tongue such bridle, O,
You're absent from your dwelling place, disorderly and idle, O.
Your hoary locks will not avail, nor your sublime oration, O,
For Grattan's Act will you transport, by your own information,
Goat: [O.'
'This parish and this neighbourhood are peaceful, quiet and
[tranquil, O;
There's no disturbance here, thank God, and may it long
[continue so.
Your oath I don't regard a pin, to sign for my committal, O,
For my jury will be gentlemen, to grant me an acquittal, O.'
Peeler:
'I'll soon chastise your impudence and insolvent behaviour, O;
Well bound to Cashel you'll be sent, where you will find no
[favour, O.
Impartial Billy Purefoy will sign your condemnation, O,
And from there to Cork you will be sent for speedy
Goat: [transportation, O.'
'The Penal Laws I ne'er trangressed, by need or combination, O;
I have no fixed place of abode, nor certain habitation, O.
Bansha is my dwelling-place, where I was bred and born, O,
Descended from an honest race, therefore your threats I scorn, O.

Peeler:
'Let the consequence be what it will, a peeler's power I'll let you
[know!
I'll fetter you at all events and march you off to prison, O.
You villain! sure you can't deny before a judge and jury, O,
That I on you found two long spears which threatened me with
Goat: [fury, O.'
'I'm certain if you weren't drunk with whiskey, rum or brandy,
[O,
You would not have such gallant spuuk, or be so bold or manly, O.
You readily would let me pass if I'd the sterling handy, O,
To treat you to a poteen glass – O, 'tis then I'd be the dandy, O!'

Come, fill us up a flowing bowl! we'll drink a grand libation, O,
And toast a health to each true son throughout this grand old
[nation, O!
We'll toast brave Ireland three times three, with pride and
[acclamation, O;
May all her people be made free by speedy separation, O!

Sir Robert Peel was appointed Secretary of Ireland by the
British Government in 1812, and one of his first acts was to form
a police force. The presence of such a force today seems to us
necessary, even vital, for the maintenance of law and order, but
at that time it was a new idea: and in Ireland particularly, as just
another interference with the peoples liberty by the occupying
power. The members of the new force were quickly labelled
'Peelers' and 'Bobbies' after their creator, and were the subject
of ridicule, particularly when their authority to arrest and detain
for small offences became apparent. Darby Ryan of Bansha, a
small village half-way on the road between Cahir and Tipperary
Town, contributed much to the ridicule when he wrote this song
well over a century ago, for within a short time it was being sung
in a wide district around. It is said to have been inspired by some
of the new force taking some straying goats who were causing an
obstruction into 'custody.'

Songs of Love and Courtin'

35. KITTY OF COLERAINE

A dainty song from the North – and an old one, for it certainly goes back to the 18th century. The very air is roguish. It is a splendid song for a light tenor with a lilt in his voice.

KITTY OF COLERAINE

*Words: unknown**
Air: 'Kitty of Coleraine'

As beautiful Kitty one morning was tripping,
With a pitcher of milk from the fair of Coleraine,
When she saw me she stumbled, the pitcher it tumbled,
And all the sweet butter milk water'd the plain.
'Oh, what shall I do now?' Twas looking at you now!
Sure, sure, such a pitcher I'll ne'er meet again!
'Twas the pride of my dairy; O Barney McCleary,
You're sent as a plague to the girls of Coleraine'.

I sat down beside her, and gently did chide her,
That such a misfortune should give her such pain;
A kiss then I gave her, and, before I did leave her,
She vowed, for such pleasure, she'd break it again.
'Twas hay-making season; I can't tell the reason,
Misfortune will never come single, 'tis plain;
For very soon after poor Kitty's disaster
The devil a pitcher was whole in Coleraine.

* The song has been attributed to Edward Lysaght, but it is by no means certain that he wrote it.

36. DANCE LIGHT, FOR MY HEART LIES UNDER YOUR FEET, LOVE

A charmingly lilting song redolent of the skirl of the Irish piper and the moon shining on the dancers at the crossroad; by the same author of the equally charming 'Spinning Wheel' who originated from County Limerick.

DANCE LIGHT, FOR MY HEART IT LIES UNDER YOUR FEET, LOVE

Words: John F. Waller, LL.D.
Air: 'Hush the cat from under the table'

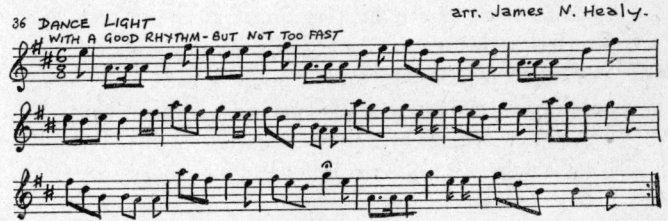

36 DANCE LIGHT
WITH A GOOD RHYTHM - BUT NOT TOO FAST
arr. James N. Healy.

'Ah, sweet Kitty Neil, rise up from that wheel –
Your neat little foot will be weary from spinning;
Come trip down with me to the sycamore tree,
Half the parish is there, and the dance is beginning.
The sun is gone down, but the full harvest moon
Shines sweetly and cool on the dew-whitened valley;
While all the air rings with the soft, loving things,
Each little bird sings in the green shaded alley.'

With a blush and a smile, Kitty rose up the while,
Her eyes in the glass, as she bound her hair, glancing;
'Tis hard to refuse when a young lover sues –
So she couldn't but choose to go off to the dancing.
And now on the green, the glad groups are seen –
Each gay-hearted lad with the lass of his choosing;
And Pat, without fail, leads our sweet Kitty Neil –
Somehow, when he asked, she ne'er thought of refusing.

93

Now, Felix Magee puts his pipes to his knee,
And, with flourish so free, sets each couple in motion;
With a cheer and a bound, the lads patter the ground –
The maids move around just like swans on the ocean.
Cheeks bright as the rose – feet light as the doe's,
Now coyly retiring, now boldly advancing –
Search the world all round, from the sky to the ground,
No such sight can be found as an Irish lass dancing!

Sweet Kate! who could view your bright eyes of deep blue,
Beaming humidly through their dark lashes so mildly,
Your fair-turned arm, heaving breast, rounded form,
Nor feel his heart warm, and his pulses throb wildly?
Young Pat feels his heart, as he gazes, depart,
Subdued by the smart of such painful yet sweet love;
The sight leaves his eye, as he cries with a sigh,
'Dance light, for my heart it lies under your feet, love!'

A mock-mournful song about the lover who sacrificed all (even his breeches) for an ungrateful sweet one. Be careful when singing it solo: it must sound a little puzzled, and wistful, but it can be dreary if it is sung too slow. With a nice lilt however, it is a grand ballad, with a nice twist of humour.

It hardly came from the peasant class about which it is written, for an Irish countryman would hardly admit to the implied lack of legal knowledge: he would argue his way out of it, come what may!: but then many of the ballads of mid-19th century were written by gentile versifiers rather than by those of the soil.

PURTY MOLLY BRALLAGHAN

Words: unknown
Air: 'Molly Brallaghan'

Ah! then, ma'am, dear, did you never hear of purty Molly
                                       [Brallaghan?
Troth, dear, I've lost her, and I'll never be a man again;
Not a spot on my hide will the summer's sun e'er tan agin,
Since Molly she has left me all alone to die.
The place where my heart was you might easy roll a turnip in,
It's the size of all Dublin, and from Dublin to the Divil's Glin;
If she choose to take another, sure she might have sent mine back
And not to leave me here all alone for to die!   [again

Ma'am, dear, I remember when the milking time was past and
                                         [gone,
We went into the meadows, where she swore I was the only man
That ever she could love – yet, oh! the base, the cruel one,
After all that to leave me here alone to die!
Ma'am, dear, I remember as we came home the rain began;
I rolled her in my frieze coat, tho' the divil a waiscot I had on,
And my shirt was rather fine-drawn; yet, oh! the base and cruel
After all that she's left me here alone for to die!   [one,

I went and told my tale to Father M'Donnell, ma'am,
And then I went and ax'd advice of Councillor O'Connell,
[ma'am.
He told me promise-breeches had been ever since the world
[began –
Now, I have only one pair, ma'am, and they are corduroy!
Arrah! what could he mean, ma'am, or what would you advise
[me to?
Must my corduroys to Molly go? – in troth I'm bothered what
[to do.
I can't afford to lose both my heart and my breeches, too;
Yet what need I care when I've only to die!

Oh! the left side of my carcase is as weak as water gruel, ma'am,
The divil a bit upon my bones since Molly's proved so cruel,
I wish I had a carbine, I'd go and fight a duel, ma'am – [ma'am.
Sure it's better for to kill myself than stay here to die!
I'm hot and determined as a live salamander, ma'am;
Won't you come to my wake when I go my long meander,
[ma'am?
Oh! I feel myself as valiant as the famous Alexander, ma'am,
When I hear ye cryin' round me, 'Arrah! why did you die?'

A comic and rueful song. Whereas the victim of Molly Bralla-ghan is mournful at his lack of success with his beloved, Dan is not so sure that his success is going to be worth while – particularly if it means that when he wins the daughter, Ma comes too! These semi-reluctant songs about courting, which often in the country in Ireland was a family arranged affair, are frequent enough, but few have the originality of Dan's conversation with his prospective mother-in-law, which gradually loses enthusiasm as her complacent demands on him grow larger. There is a rather more violent and definite end used to the song by some singers, when his final retort is 'I will in me A ... says Dan'', and while this may not be altogether successful on the concert platform, I have heard it used with fair effect in the drawing-room when the emphasis is not too violent.

A most effective song when performed by the singer with the right personality.

'THANK YOU MA'AM' SAYS DAN
Words and Music: traditional

'What brought you in to my room, to my room, to my room?
What brought you in to my room,' says the mistress unto Dan.
'I came here to court your daughter Ma'am
I thought it no great harm ma'am'
'Oh! Dan, my dear you're welcome here',
'I thank you ma'am', says Dan.

'How come you to know my daughter, my daughter, my
[daughter?
How come you to know my daughter?' says the mistress unto
'Goin' to the well for water, ma'am,   [Dan.
To raise the can I taught her ma'am',
Oh! Dan, my dear, you're welcome here
'I thank you ma'am' says Dan.

'Oh! then you can have my daughter, my daughter, my daughter,
I'll let you take my daughter,' says the mistress unto Dan.
'And when you take my daughter, Dan,
Of course you will take me also, Dan.
Oh! Dan, my dear you're welcome here',
'I thank you ma'am' says Dan.

This couple they got married, got married, got married,
This couple they got married, Miss Elizabeth and Dan.
And now he keeps her mother and her father and his charmer, O,
And they're known throughout the country
By the name of 'Thank ye, Ma'am'.

39. THE ONE-EYED RILEY

A gay song, and a pretty bawdy one in one military version not
printed here, of which Dr. Rabelais might have approved,
although the printer wouldn't! The lover takes his cares lightly,
and his formidable father-in-law in his stride.

From the time of the volunteers, and particularly through
Napoleonic times a great number of Irishmen served in the
British Army, despite the feeling in the country, and this is one
of the songs which arose from Army life, and indeed it is redolent
of the barrack square. A good song for a bass-baritone with 'life'
in his voice.

THE ONE-EYED RILEY

Words and Music: unknown

As I was sittin' by the fire
Atin' spuds and drinkin' porter
Suddenly a thought came into me head
I'd like to marry oul' Riley's daughter

Chorus:
Giddy-I-ay. Giddy-I-ay, Giddy-I-ay for the one-eyed Riley
Rub-a-dub-a-dub, (pause) Play it on your big bass drum.

For Riley played on the big bass drum
Riley had a mind for murder and slaughter
He had one bright red glittering eye
And he kept that eye on his lovely daughter.
Chorus

One night when Riley was in bed
I crept up to her room and caught her
Took her safely off to wed
Quick as a flash, with oul' Riley's daughter.
Chorus

I got me a ring and a parson too,
I got me a 'Scratch' in the married quarter:
Settled me down to a peaceful life,
As happy as a king with O'Riley's daughter.
Chorus

Suddenly a footstep on the stair
Who should it be but the one-eyed Riley
With two pistols in his hand
Lookin' for the man who married his daughter.
Chorus

I took oul' Riley be the hair
Shoved his head in a pail of water
Fired his pistols into the air
A damn sight quicker than I married his daughter.
Chorus

A bouncing song, which again is about the man who has regrets that the courting was successful! Keep it swinging.

PATSY MC CANN

There's a man by the name of Mike Hogan
Who's plague-in' me out of me life,
He has a big daughter named Brigit
And he wants me to make her me wife.
She stands six foot four in her stockings
Her waist of me-self would make three
And whenever I'm standing beside her
Me elbows just reach to her knees.

Chorus:
Patsy Mc Cann will you marry me daughter,
Oh! Patsy Mc Cann is the girl you'll wed;
Ten golden sovereigns down I will give you,
A three legged stool and a fine feather bed.
Saint Peter, Saint Paul and Saint Paterick
All the pictures that hang on the wall,
I'll throw them all into the bargain,
If you'll marry my daughter at all.

Well I married that big Brigit Hogan
And she's mine now for better or worse,
But the blessing that she should have brought me
Would appear to have changed a curse.
She strikes me and bites me and flays me
She ties me lest I run away,
This six foot four beauty's a caution
But her father was worse for to say: –
Chorus:

41. KELLY, THE BOY FROM KILLANNE

The Wexford rising of 1798 caused many fine ballads to be written; at the time, and for long after: and no collection would be complete without at least one of them. This stirring song breathes the very spirit of the time.

John Kelly was the son of a well-to-do merchant in Killanne which is a small town in the barony of Bantry (Co. Wexford), but although his name is remembered with pride, very little is really known about his exploits. It can be said that he was a leader of the men of his district: that his party joined the insurgents after the taking of Enniscorthy; that he was a leader of the party which cut off and defeated a party of reinforcements on their way to Wexford. He fought subsequently at Wexford, and was badly wounded while gallantly leading his men at New Ross. From there he was carried back to Wexford, and when that town was re-taken by the military he was taken and hanged, with little more than an apology for a trial. After death his head was kicked around the street by the soldiery.

In fact the ballad tells the story, in a concise summary, of the action in the Southern part of the county, during the brief hour of glory enjoyed by the insurgent forces.

'Brave Harvey' is Bagenal Harvey, a Protestant landowner who was commander of the rebel forces at New Ross.

Another splendid ballad by the same writer on the period, 'Boulavogue', commemorating the exploits of Father John Murphy, and the famous song about 'the Croppy Boy' (most of the insurgents were known as 'Croppies' because of the way in which their hair was cut) will be found in the first Book of Ballads; and there are many, many others on Wolfe Tone and on those who fought in Wexford, Wicklow and the North in the time of the United Irishmen, as well as several, such as 'The Races of Castlebar' on the subsequent French landings in the West.

KELLY, THE BOY FROM KILLANNE

Words: P. J. MacCall
Air: P. J. Mac Call

'What's the news? What's the news? O my bold Shelmalier,
With your long-barrelled gun of the sea?
Say what wind from the sun blows his messenger here
With a hymn of the dawn for the free?'
'Goodly news, goodly news, do I bring, Youth of Forth;
Goodly news shall you hear, Bargy man!
For the Boys march at morn from the South to the North,
Led by Kelly, the Boy from Killanne!'

'Tell me who is that giant with the gold curling hair –
He who rides at the head of your band?
Seven feet is his height, with some inches to spare,
And he looks like a King in command!'
'Ah, my lads, that's the pride of the bold Shelmaliers,
'Mong our greatest of heroes, a Man! –
Fling your beavers aloft and give three ringing cheers
For John Kelly, the Boy from Killanne!'

Enniscorthy's in flames, and old Wexford is won,
And the Barrow to-morrow we cross,
On a hill o'er the town we have planted a gun
That will batter the gateways of Ross!
All the Forth men and Bargy men march o'er the heath,
With brave Harvey to lead on the van;
But the foremost of all in the grim Gap of Death
Will be Kelly, the Boy from Killanne!

But the gold sun of Freedom grew darkened at Ross,
And it set by the Slaney's red waves;
And poor Wexford, stript naked, hung high on a cross,
And her heart pierced by traitors and slaves!
Glory O! Glory O! to her brave sons who died
For the cause of long-down-trodden man!
Glory O! to Mount Leinster's own darling and pride –
Dauntless Kelly, the Boy from Killanne.

42. THE WIDOW MCGRATH

While Ballads were being written – such as the Shan Van Vocht
(Sean Bhean Bhocht – meaning 'poor old woman', i.e. Ireland) on
the help expected by the United Irishmen from Napoleon and his
forces (help which was too late and too small when it came) many
Irishmen enlisted in the forces which opposed them subsequently
in the Peninsula and at Waterloo.

The recruiting sergeant, with his drum escort, became a
familiar figure of the time, and with the desperate shortage of
men was up to many ruses to induce the country lads to take The
King's Shilling. These include encouraging the prospective
victim to imbibe a fair amount of liquor at the sergeant's expense
and then pressing the shilling into his hand when he was no
longer in a condition to resist. Once he had accepted the shilling
he was in the Army and that was an end of it. The grandfather
of Sir Arthur Sullivan, the composer, was caught in Tralee in his
way. He was one of those who left the country and never
returned: either to leave their bones on a foreign field, or to come
out of the Army and settle down for their remaining life in
England. 'Mrs. McGrath's' son was one of those who came back,
maimed, but content to be in receipt of a pension which would
ensure against bare want for his remaining days. The grimness of
the subject is combated successfully by the light treatment which
so often makes charming ballads out of what might otherwise
be difficult material. A very old ballad, widespread on the East
coast particularly.

Words and Music: Traditional
(early 19 th century)

Oh! the widow McGrath lived in Kilrush,
And she had the money very flush
She had one son her darlin' dear
And he went to list for a fusilier

Chorus:
With me whacks-fol-de-lol: fol-de-lol-de-lay
Whacks-fol-de-lol, fol-de-lol, de-lay.
With me whacks-fol-de-lol, fol-de-lol-de-lay
Whacks fol-de-lol, fol-de-lol, de-lay.

'Oh, Mrs. McGrath' the sergeant said
'Wouldn't you make a soldier out of your son Ted'
'With a fine red coat and a three-cocked-hat,
'And now Mrs. McGrath, wouldn't you like that?'

Mrs. McGrath waited on the shore
For the space of seven long years or more
'Till she saw a big ship comin' over to the quay
Says Mrs. McGrath, 'Clear outa' me way'.

'Now were you mad' and were you blind
That you left your two fine legs behind
And was it from walking over the say
That you wore your two shin-bones away.'

'Oh I was not mad, and I was not blind
When I left my two shin-bones behind
But a big cannon ball, on the twelfth of May
Came and whipped me two fine legs away.'

'Great mighty wars I will proclaim
'Gainst the King of France, and the King of Spain
And I will make them rue the day
That they stole me son's fine legs away.'

'Arrah, mother, ma'am, don't take on so,
I got fifty pounds for every toe,
And if I had another pair
I'd be off to the wars and lave 'em there.

43. THE GLENDALOUGH SAINT

St. Kevin, the legendary Saint of Glendalough in Co. Wicklow, gets somewhat scant respect in this old ballad; but the disrespect smells more of affection than impiety. It seems to say – how could any healthy young country girl understand that a fellow wanted to live by himself in a cave?

THE GLENDALOUGH SAINT

Words and Music:
Traditional (Midlands)

At Glendalough lived a great saint
Who was famous for deeds of austerity.
His manners was curious and quaint
For on girls he looked with asperity.
He was fond of readin' a book
When he got one quite to his wishes,
But was fonder of castin' a hook
And spent many a day anglin' for fishes,
Right foldidle doldidle dol,
Right foldidle doldidle addy,
Right foldidle doldidle dol,
Right foldidle doldidle addy.

But as he was fishin' one day
A catchin' some kind of a trout, sir,
Young Kathleen was walkin' that way,
Just to see what the saint was about, sir
'You're a mighty fine fisher' says Kate
'Tis yourself is the boy that can hook them
But when you have caught them so nate,
Don't you want some young woman to cook them?'
Right foldidle doldidle dol, etc.

'Be gone out of that' said the saint,
'For I am a man of great piety,
Me character I wouldn't taint
By keeping such class of society'.
But Kathleen wasn't goin' to give in
For when he got home to his rockery
He found her sittin' there in,
A-polishing up of her crockery
Right foldidle doldidle dol, etc.

He gave the poor creature a shake,
Oh! I wish that the peelers had caught him;
He threw her right into the lake,
And of course she sank down to the bottom.
It is rumoured from that very day,
Kathleen's ghost can be seen on the river;
And the saint never raised up his hand,
For he died of the right kind of fever.
Right foldidle doldidle dol, etc.

44. THE FINDING OF MOSES

This nonsensical historical comment needs the genuine Dublin twang to put it over successfully, and it is then very amusing indeed. Imitation is hardly enough, for this in its way is a satire on balladry, and as such needs the spirit of the dry humour of the place where it was born.

THE FINDING OF MOSES
Words and Music: traditional (Dublin area)
attributed to Mc. Moran ('zozimus')

Oh! come all ye bold geographers, and listen to a lay
That I have got about a spot as is many miles away
Sure it's not about sweet Gurtin or the flower of county Down
But a foreign place contiguese to King Pharaoh's native town.

At a spot in Egypt's land that's right convenient to the Nile,
Old Pharaoh's daughter with her maids went out to bathe in style,
'Oh! come now strip off me duds', says she, and that was speedy
[done,
It was gettin' them stuck on again that used to start the fun.

When her wrappin's were removed and she prepared to face her
She made a playful leap and gave her lily hands a wave,   [bathe
But her foot caught on a cactus sprig growin' from the virgin sod,
And the yell she gave would from the grave raise up the sons of
[Nod.

Well, when she found her depth she tramped her back unto the
And for to dry her royal pelt she ran along the sand,   [land
Till stumbling by a bulrush clump and lookin' down she found
There a starin' smilin' baby in a basket on the ground.

She was desperate fond of childer as was more than plain to see,
For she cried, 'Sweet babe, this Nile you'll have, and come along
[with me';
As a child and mild and always wild her wish did not deny,
And tho' young in speech within its reach it had a powerful cry.

Oh! all back then in the palace Pharaoh said 'Whats this, me
[child'
'Sure I call him Moses, sir', she said, 'for I took him from the
[Nile';
Poor old Pharaoh got discoloured and the maids stood in a hush,
'Ah! that's new to me' says Pharaoh, 'what about the gooseberry
[bush'.

'Whose child is this?' she cried and raised her royal eyes aloft,
But her maids just sniffed and winked their eyes and said
[you're queer and soft';
And they made no more palaver till she screeched out queer and
[wild,
'Ah! Now tearin' ages tell me now which one of yiz owns the
[child'.

Sporting

The Irish are a great race for sport and play. I suppose with play most of us would include courtin', some songs of which have gone before! – and sport is almost invariably connected with horses and greyhounds. Following then are a couple of ballads on sport, the first one being an old ballad rather similar to the County Limerick Buck Hunt which was included in the Munster ballads, and a second a ballad about that most typical form of Irish racing – the local Point-to-Point.

45. THE KILRUDDERY HUNT

Words: Thomas Mozeen
Air: Sheila na Guira

A song of the chase, similar to 'The County Limerick Buck Hunt' on page 81, but dealing with the district around Dublin. It was written about the same time too, and it will be readily seen how the built up area has extended in the last two hundred years. One could hardly imagine chasing a fox thro' Monkstown nowadays!

THE KILRUDDERY HUNT

In seventeen hundred and forty-four,
The fifth of December, I think 'twas no more,
At five in the morning, by most of the clocks,
We rode from Kilruddery in search of a fox.
The Loughlinstown landlord, the brave Owen Bray,
And Johnny Adair, too, were with us that day;
Joe Debil, Hal Preston, those huntsmen so stout –
Dick Holmes, some few others, and so we set out.

We cast off our hounds for an hour or more,
When Wanton set up a most tuneable roar;
'Hark, Wanton,' cried Joe, and the rest were not slack;
For Wanton's no trifler esteemed by the pack;
Old Bounty and Collier came readily in,
And every hound joined in the musical din:
Had Diana been there, she'd been pleased to the life,
And one of the lads got a goddess to wife.

Ten minutes past nine was the time of the day
When Reynard broke cover, and this was his way –
As strong from Killegar, as if he could fear none,
Away he brush'd round by the house of Kilternan,
To Carrickmines thence, and to Cherrywood then,
Steep Shankhill he climbed, and to Ballyman glen,
Bray Common he crossed, leap'd Lord Anglesey's wall,
And seemed to say, 'Little I care for you all.'

He ran Bushes Grove up to Carbury Byrnes –
Joe Debil, Hal Preston, kept leading by turns;
The earth it was open, yet he was so stout,
Tho' he might have got in, still he chose to keep out;
To Malpas high hills was the way that he flew,
At Dalkey's stone common we had him in view;
He drove on to Bullock, he slunk Glenageary,
And so on to Monkstown, where Larry grew weary.

Thro' Rochestown wood like an arrow he passed,
And came to the steep hills of Dalkey at last;
There gallantly plunged himself into the sea,
And said in his heart, 'None can now follow me.'
But soon, to his cost, he perceived that no bounds
Could stop the pursuit of the staunch-mettled hounds.
His policy here did not serve him a rush,
Five couple of Tartars were hard at his brush.

To recover the shore then again was his drift;
But ere he could reach to the top of the clift,
He found both of speed and of daring a lack,
Being waylaid and killed by the rest of the pack.
At his death there were present the lads I have sung,
Save Larry, who, riding a garron, was flung:
Thus ended at length a most delicate chase,
That held us five hours and ten minutes' space.

Johnny Adair, was the son of Robin Adair, famous from another song.

46. SWEET MARIE

This charming ballad of Percy French has somehow not gained as much notice as some of his others. The feelings of the gentleman farmer who is left in the grass at the Point-to-Point watching the flying hooves of his hope disappearing in the distance is well portrayed; but the owner takes his loss philosophically. It is all here for those who have been to an Irish country meeting – the smell of the grass churned up by the horses, feet; the shouts of the bookies mingling with the raucous endeavours of the side show men to gain attention for their thimble riggings or three card tricks; the binoculars, the shooting sticks, and picnic lunches; stout being drunk from bottles in the refreshment tent. All part of a wonderful time when the day is fine – an Irish Point-to-Point with the race for the Farmer's Cup next on the programme.

SWEET MARIE

Words: Percy French
Air: Traditional American Tune

I've a little racin' mare called Sweet Marie,
And the temper of a bear has Sweet Marie.
But I've backed the mare to win, and on her I've all my tin,
So we'll take a trial spin, Sweet Marie.
Hould your hoult, Sweet Marie,
If you bolt, Sweet Marie,
Sure, you'll never win the Farmers' Cup for me;
And if you don't pull it through, faith, I'm done, and so are you,
For I'll trade you off for glue, Sweet Marie.

Now, the colours that I chose for Sweet Marie
Were lavender and rose for Sweet Marie,
Och, but now, no thanks to you, sure I'm quite another hue,
For I'm only black and blue, Sweet Marie,
Hould your hoult, Sweet Marie,
If you bolt, Sweet Marie,
Sure, you'll never win the Farmers' Cup for me.
Every daisy in the dell ought to know me mighty well,
For on every one I fell, Sweet Marie.

Now we're started for the Cup, my Sweet Marie
Weight for age and owners up, my Sweet Marie
Owners up, just now I own, but the way you're waltzing roun'
Sure, 'twill soon be owners down, Sweet Marie.
Hould your hoult, Sweet Marie:
Pass the colt, Sweet Marie.
Och, you've gone and lost the Farmers' Cup for me.
You're a stayer too, I find: but you're not the proper kind
For you stay too far behind, Sweet Marie.

Travel

Travelling in Ireland has taken numerous forms – the pony and trap was probably the neatest and the jarvey car (Ben the Coachman is a song about jarvies) the most picturesque. Railways came to Ireland in the middle of the 19th century, and the branch lines now unfortunately being closed down became a recognised part of the scene with the loads of people being carried to Cork on the shopping days and to Limerick, and Dublin, and the other big centres. Some of these branch lines had characteristics of their own, and one such was the West Clare line. Percy French commemorated his journey on this celebrated, but leisurely line in the ballad 'Are ye right there Michael.' Here it is – what do you think of it? or did you ever travel in similar fashion in your own district?

47. ARE YE RIGHT THERE, MICHAEL?
Words and Music: Percy French

A lay of the Wild West Clare
You may talk of Columbus's sailing
Across the Atlantical sea
But he never tried to go railing
From Ennis as far as Kilkee.
You run for the train in the mornin',
The excursion train starting at eight,
You're there when the clock gives the warnin',
And there for an hour you'll wait.
Spoken:
And as you're waiting in the train,
You'll hear the guard sing this refrain: –

'Are ye right there, Michael? are ye right?
Do you think that we'll be there before the night?
Ye've been so long in startin',
That ye couldn't say for sartin' –
Still ye might now, Michael, so ye might!'

They find out where the engine's been hiding,
And it drags you to sweet Corofin;
Says the guard, 'Back her down on the siding
There's the goods from Kilrush comin' in.'
Perhaps it comes in in two hours,
Perhaps it breaks down on the way;
'If it does,' says the guard, 'be the powers
We're here for the rest of the day!'

Spoken:
And while you sit and curse your luck,
The train backs down into a truck!

'Are ye right there, Michael, are you right?
Have ye got the parcel there for Mrs. White?
Ye haven't! Oh, Begorra!
Say it's comin' down to-morra –
And it might now, Michael, so it might!'

At Lahinch the sea shines like a jewel,
With joy you are ready to shout,
When the stoker cries out, 'There's no fuel,
And the fire's taytotally out.
But hand up that bit of a log there –
I'll soon have ye out of the fix;
There's a fine clamp of turf in the bog there;'
And the rest go a-gatherin' sticks.
Spoken:
And while you're breakin' bits of trees,
You hear some wise remarks like these: –

'Are ye right there, Michael? are ye right?
Do ye think ye can get the fire to light?'
'Oh, an hour you'll require,
For the turf-it might be drier –'
'Well, it might now, Michael, so it might'

Kilkee! Oh, you never get near it!
You're in luck if the train brings you back,
For the permanent way is so queer, it
Spends most of its time off the track,
Uphill the ould engin' is climbin',
While the passengers push with a will;
You're in luck when you reach Ennistymon,
For all the way home is down-hill.

Spoken:
And as you're wobbling through the dark,
You hear the guard make this remark: –

'Are ye right there, Michael? are ye right?
Do you think that ye'll be home before it's light?'
''Tis all dependin' whether
The ould engin' holds together –'
'And it might now, Michael, so it might!'

This song of the West Clare Railway, which used to slowly
meander its way over the beautiful coastline from Ennis to Kilkee
nearly landed the author in court shortly after it was written.

The owners of the railway felt they had been 'taken for a ride'
and entered a claim against French for libel, but before the case
got to court it was withdrawn in the great entertainer's favour;
– possibly a wise decision as that gentleman's quick wit might
have added further to their discomfort if the case had gone on!

Not the best of Percy French's ballads perhaps, but a most
unusual one, and of particular historic interest with the closing
down in recent years of many of the old branch lines of the rail-

way, including the West Clare; so that the journey which Percy French undertook and perpetuated in song is now only a memory.

As mentioned earlier there are few Irish ballads about the sea – especially considering that we are a sea-girt people – and this is one of them. It is a breezy ballad and should be sung with a good swing. In some ways it could be considered as a music-hall song rather than a genuine comic ballad but has sufficient of the satirical mood to rank as a true ballad.

THE IRISH ROVER

Words: Traditional
Music: (19 th century)

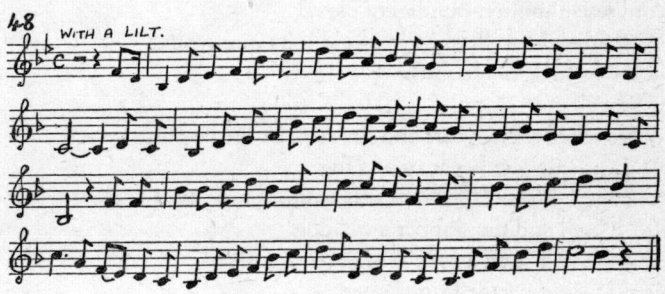

In the year of our Lord eighteen hundred and six
We set sail from the fair Cobh of Cork,
We were bound far away with a cargo of bricks
For the fair City Hall of New York.
We'd a beautiful craft, she was rigged fore and aft,
And Lord how the trade winds drove her,
As she stood to the blast, she had twenty-three masts
And we called her the Irish Rover.

Donoghue and Mac Hugh came from Red Waterloo.
And O'Neill and Mac Flail from the Rhine.
There was Ludd and Mac Gludd from the land of the flood
Pat Malone, Mike Mac Gowan and O'Brien,
Bould Mac Gee, Mac Entee and big Neill from Tigree
And Michael O'Dowd from Dover
And a man from Turkestan sure his name was Kid Mac Cann
Was the skipper of the Irish Rover.

We had one million bags of the best Sligo rags,
We had two million barrels of bones,
We had three million sides from old blind horse hides
We had four million bags full of stones.
We had five million dogs and six million hogs,
And seven million bundles of clover.
We had eight million bales of old billy goats tails,
In the hold of the Irish Rover.

O we sailed seven years and the measles broke out,
And the ship lost her way in a fog.
And the whole of the crew was reduced unto two
Just meself and the skipper's old dog.
And we struck on a rock with a terrible shock
And Lord, she rolled right over.
Turned nine times right around; the old dog he got drowned
I'm the last of the Irish Rover.
Chorus:
Fare thee well, my own true one, I'm going far from you
And I will swear by the stars above, forever I'll be true;
But as I part it will break my heart, and when the trip is over,
I'll roam again in true Irish style aboard the 'Irish Rover'.

Songs from the Irish

One of the richest sources of music in our country has been the old songs in the Irish language which very often are so ancient that the authors, or even the period in which they were lived cannot be accurately established. The melody of 'Eibhlin a Riun' (Eileen Aroon), for instance, is attributed to Carol O'Daly, a bard who lived in the 14th century; and many others may have originally been composed by the bards of the courts – or may even have been melodies already existing as traditional, and used by them: we do not know. Thomas Moore – whose name should not be decried by any Irish balladmaker, despite the stickiness of some of his work – adopted a similar method, taking the old Gaelic tunes, and preserving them for us by writing editions in English. His method, however, was not to make a near literal translation of the original song, but to write a new one on an entirely different subject which he felt the music fitted. What I have tried to do here is to present a few of these old songs in Irish – a very few of the many hundreds that exist – and give them side by side in the original Irish, and in the English translation which seems best for the voice. Other translations known to the reader may seem to him to be better poetry, but here I am thinking of the translation as something which is to be sung: and therefore have used the words which seem best for a singer in vowel sounds, enunciation, and phrasing. These translations too, seem best suited to the spirit of the original.

I deliberately call these 'songs' rather than 'ballads' as the latter is normally written to commemorate a special event or person, while these numbers are on a more general subject, – usually the universal one of love.

A recurring theme in Irish love-songs is the meeting with a beautiful young lady to whom the beholder gives his heart for ever – often in vain. Here the meeting is with a milkmaid in the

Fáinne Geal an Lae

Maidin moċ do ġabar amaċ
    Aр ḃruaċ Loċa Léin
An Samrad teaċt 'ran craoḃ le n-air
    'gur lonnra te ó'n ngréin
Ar tairdeal don tré ḃailte puirt
    'gur bánta míne ré.
Cia ġeoḃainn le'm air aċ an ċúilḟionn dear le fáinne
geal an lae.

Ní raiḃ ḃróg ná stoca cairp ná clóc
    'Aр mo stóirín óg ó'n rpéir
Aċ folt fionn órga ríor go troig
    Ag fár go barr an féir
Ḃí callán crúite 'a 'na glaic
    'San ḃrúċt ba ḋear a rġéiṁ
Do рug barr-ġean ó Ḃénur dear
    Le fáinne geal an lae.

Do fuid an ḃrídeaċ ríor le'm air
    Aр binnre glar de'n féar
Ag magad léi ḃíor d'á maoíaṁ go рrar
    Mar ṁnaoi ná rġарfainn léi
'Sé dúirt rí liom-ra "Imig uaim,
    A'r rġaoil mé ar ríul go réid
Sin iad anear na roillre 'teaċt
    Le fáinne geal an lae".

early morning by the side of Lough Leane (one of the famous lakes of Killarney). The original is graceful and wistful as it trips along to a dainty lyric, but it must be confessed that although there are many translations, few of them are really satisfactory for the voice. The one translated here is probably the best. John McCormack made a splendid recording of the song.

THE DAWNING OF THE DAY

Words: Traditional
Music:

One morning early I walked forth by the margin of Lough Leane;
The sunshine dressed the trees in green,
And summer bloomed again;
I left the town and wandered on
Through fields all green and gay;
And whom should I meet but a sweet colleen
By the dawning of the day.

No cap or cloak this maiden wore, her neck and feet were bare;
Down to the grass in ringlets fell
Her glossy golden hair;
A milking pail was in her hand
She was lovely, young and gay;
She bore the palm from Venus bright,
By the dawning of the day.

On a mossy bank I sat me down,
With the maiden by my side;
With gentle words I courted her,
And asked her to be my bride;
She said, 'young man don't bring me blame,
But let me go away,
For morning's light is shining bright,
By the dawning of the day.'

This number has been ascribed to Carol O'Daly, a bard in the 14th century, and with its rising and falling cadence is a typical, and splendid example of a sorrowful Irish melody with its gentle flow. With a little imagination one can picture it sung to the harp in the courts of centuries ago; but it is in essence a song of reflection for the solitary singer, thinking of his absent love.

The translation here given is by Gerald Griffen, one of the Cork poets, who wrote the 'Collegians' from which was taken the story of 'The Colleen Bawn' for Boucicaults play, and Benedicts Opera – 'The Lily of Killarney.' Later he embraced the religious life and became a Christian Brother.

Eibhlín a Rúin

Le grádh duit níl radharc am ceann, Eibhlín a Rúin
Is trácht ort is radhbhreas liom, Eibhlín a Rúin
Ó mo mhórdháil ró-ghreidhmheas tú, rólár na Soillre'r tú
Ó mo lile tú, mo mheidhir is tú, mo bhruinneal tú go
    deimhin.
A'r mo chlár dá bhfuil ra coill reo'r tú
A'r mo chroí 'rtig níl leigheas gan tú, Eibhlín a Rúin.

Le cúirtéir na tlúig béit, is tú, Eibhlín a Rúin
Dúirt bhréag nú'r liam fémig tú, Eibhlín a Rúin
Mar is breátha ná Bénur tú, 'ris áilne ná'n Réilteantú
Ó mo Hélen tú gan béim is tú mo rór, mo lil mo chraobh
Mo rtór d'á bhfuil ra traol ro'r tú
Agur rún mo chroí agur mo cléib is tú Eibhlín a Rúin.

EILEEN AROON

Words: Gerald Griffin
Music: Irish air

When, like the early rose,
Eileen aroon!
Beauty in childhood blows;
Eileen aroon!
When like a diadem,
Buds blush around the stem,
Which is the fairest gem?
Eileen aroon!

Is it the laughing eye,
Eileen aroon!
Is it the timid sigh,
Eileen aroon!
Is it the tender tone,
Soft as the string'd harp's moan?
Oh, it is the truth alone.
Eileen Aroon!

When, like the rising day,
Eileen aroon!
Love sends his early ray,
Eileen aroon!
What makes his dawning glow
Changeless through joy or woe?
Only the constant know –
Eileen aroon!

I knew a valley fair,
Eileen aroon!
I knew a cottage there,
Eileen aroon!
Far in that valley's shade,
I knew a gentle maid,
Flower of a hazel glade,
Eileen aroon!

A lovely Irish melody; a love-song of high degree. The translation is by Dr. George Petrie, who for a long time before his death in 1866 rendered great service to Irish music by his collections of old music and songs.

Péarla an Brollaig Báin

Tá cailín deas am ċrá le bliain 'gur le lá
A'r ní feadaim a fáil le bréagaḋ
Níl airte clis le ná ḋá ġcanaiḋ fir le mná
Nár ċaiteamar gan táċt léi-re
Do'n bFrainnc nó do'n Spáinn ḋá dtéaḋ maġná
Do ragainn-re gaċ lá ḋá féaċaint.
A'r mara ḋúinn-ne tá sé i nḋán
An annir ċiúin seo d'fáil
Mac Muire na nGrás d'ár saoraḋ.

'Sa cailín cáilce bláiṫ ḋá dtugar searc a'r grá
Ná tabair-re gaċ tráṫ ḋam éarsaḋ
'Sa liaċt annir mín im ḋéaiḋ le buaiḋ
A'r maoin 'na láiṁ
Ḋá ngaḃaimír it áit-re céile
Póg a'r míle fáilte a'r barrai geal do láiṁ
Sé an-iarrfainn go bráċ mar sspéaleaċ.
A'r mara ḋam-ra daoire indán
A péarla an Brollaig Báin
Nár ṫí mire slán ó'n Aonaċ.

Words: translated by George Petrie
Air: Pearla an bhrollaig bhain

There's a colleen fair as May
For a year and for a day
I have sought by ev'ry way
Her heart to gain.

There's no art of tongue or eye
Fond youths with maidens try,
But I've tried with ceaseless sigh,
Yet tried in vain.

If to far-off France or Spain
She crossed the raging main,
Her face to see again
The seas I'd brave.

But if 'tis Heaven's decree
That mine she may not be,
May the Son of Mary me
In mercy save.

Oh, thou blooming milk-white dove
To whom I've given my love,
Do not ever thus reprove
My constancy.

There are maidens would be mine
With wealth in land and kine,
If my heart would but incline
To turn from thee.

But a kiss with welcome bland
And touch of thy fair hand,
Is all that I demand,
Would'st thou not spurn.

For if not mine, dear girl,
Oh, snowy-breasted pearl,
May I never from the fair
With life return.

INDEX TO FIRST LINES